The Object Lessons serie
to magic: the books take
and animate them with
political struggle, science, and popular mythology. Filled
with fascinating details and conveyed in sharp, accessible
prose, the books make the everyday world come to life.
Be warned: once you've read a few of these, you'll start
walking around your house, picking up random objects,
and musing aloud: 'I wonder what the story is behind
this thing?'"

Steven Johnson, author of *Where Good Ideas
Come From* and *How We Got to Now*

Object Lessons describes themselves as 'short, beautiful
books,' and to that, I'll say, amen. . . . If you read enough
Object Lessons books, you'll fill your head with plenty of
trivia to amaze and annoy your friends and loved ones—
caution recommended on pontificating on the objects
surrounding you. More importantly, though . . . they
inspire us to take a second look at parts of the everyday
that we've taken for granted. These are not so much
lessons about the objects themselves, but opportunities
for self-reflection and storytelling. They remind us that
we are surrounded by a wondrous world, as long as we
care to look.'"

John Warner, *The Chicago Tribune*

"In 1957 the French critic and semiotician Roland Barthes published *Mythologies*, a groundbreaking series of essays in which he analysed the popular culture of his day, from laundry detergent to the face of Greta Garbo, professional wrestling to the Citroën DS. This series of short books, Object Lessons, continues the tradition."

Melissa Harrison, *Financial Times*

"Though short, at roughly 25,000 words apiece, these books are anything but slight."

Marina Benjamin, *New Statesman*

"The Object Lessons project, edited by game theory legend Ian Bogost and cultural studies academic Christopher Schaberg, commissions short essays and small, beautiful books about everyday objects from shipping containers to toast. *The Atlantic* hosts a collection of 'mini object-lessons'. . . . More substantive is Bloomsbury's collection of small, gorgeously designed books that delve into their subjects in much more depth."

Cory Doctorow, *Boing Boing*

The joy of the series . . . lies in encountering the various turns through which each of their authors has been put by his or her object. The object predominates, sits squarely center stage, directs the action. The object decides the genre, the chronology, and the limits of the study. Accordingly, the author has to take her cue from the *thing* she chose or that chose her. The result is a wonderfully uneven series of books, each one a *thing* unto itself."

Julian Yates, *Los Angeles Review of Books*

. . . edifying and entertaining . . . perfect for slipping in a pocket and pulling out when life is on hold."

Sarah Murdoch, *Toronto Star*

. . . a sensibility somewhere between Roland Barthes and Wes Anderson."

Simon Reynolds, author of *Retromania: Pop Culture's Addiction to Its Own Past*

OBJECTLESSONS

A book series about the hidden lives of ordinary things.

Series Editors:

Ian Bogost and Christopher Schaberg

Advisory Board:

Sara Ahmed, Jane Bennett, Jeffrey Jerome Cohen, Johanna Drucker, Raiford Guins, Graham Harman, renée hoogland, Pam Houston, Eileen Joy, Douglas Kahn, Daniel Miller, Esther Milne, Timothy Morton, Kathleen Stewart, Nigel Thrift, Rob Walker, Michele White.

In association with

BOOKS IN THE SERIES

rust

JEAN-MICHEL RABATÉ

BLOOMSBURY ACADEMIC
NEW YORK · LONDON · OXFORD · NEW DELHI · SYDNEY

BLOOMSBURY ACADEMIC
Bloomsbury Publishing Inc
1385 Broadway, New York, NY 10018, USA

BLOOMSBURY, BLOOMSBURY ACADEMIC and the Diana logo
are trademarks of Bloomsbury Publishing Plc

First published in the United States of America 2018

Cover design: Alice Marwick

Library of Congress Cataloging-in-Publication Data
Names: Rabaté, Jean-Michel, 1949- author.
Title: Rust / Jean-Michel Rabaté.
Description: New York, NY, USA: Bloomsbury Academic, an imprint of
Bloomsbury Publishing Inc., 2018. | Series: Object lessons | Includes
bibliographical references and index.
Identifiers: LCCN 2017043797 (print) | LCCN 2017045499 (ebook)
| ISBN 9781501329500 (ePDF) | ISBN 9781501329517 (ePub) |
ISBN 9781501329494 (pbk.: alk. paper)
Subjects: LCSH: Metals–Social aspects. | Corrosion and anti-
corrosives–Philosophy. | Metals in literature. | Oxidation–Philosophy. |
Ferric oxide–Social aspects.
Classification: LCC TA418.74 (ebook) | LCC TA418.74 .R324 2018 (print) |
DDC 620.1/1223–dc23
LC record available at https://lccn.loc.gov/2017043797

ISBN: PB: 978-1-5013-2949-4
ePDF: 978-1-5013-2950-0
eBook: 978-1-5013-2951-7

Series: Object Lessons

Typeset by Deanta Global Publishing Services, Chennai, India
Printed and bound in the United States of America

To find out more about our authors and books visit www.bloomsbury.com
and sign up for our newsletters.

CONTENTS

INTRODUCTION

The word "rust" always brought me a strange form of satisfaction. The roots of my fascination with a phenomenon that most people see as an annoyance or decay go back to my childhood. When I was five, in Bordeaux, my family moved into a stately but decrepit house with a long, zigzagging garden. Built at the turn of the century, the place needed repairs. We hired a genial painter called Henri Talon. He first tackled the huge oak shutters whose peeling paint had not been refreshed in over fifty years. The first time I saw Monsieur Talon, he was in our garden with black goggles, directing a blowtorch at wooden shutters laid out on rickety trestles. Impressed by the blue flame and the pungent smell of paint and oil fumes, I questioned: "Why are you frying our shutters?" Laughing, he lifted his goggles, twitched his droopy moustache, and began a Homeric tirade I have since never forgotten.

Talon explained the difference between wood, a noble material, and iron, a treacherous one. Iron looks sturdy on the surface, but it is weaker than it seems. Oak planks, once repainted, would be like new; metal parts, iron hinges, fasteners, latches, and chains—these are all problems. These needed to be unscrewed, cleaned with metal brushes, dipped in acid solutions, and given a special anticorrosion layer before finally being repainted. Talon showed me where an old, pinkish undercoat had become brittle and practically dissolved, disclosing patches of rotten, spongy iron. Oak wood, once sanded, would be pristine—but with fickle iron, one must be on guard against the return of rust. *La rouille!* It was the first time I heard the word. Given Talon's dramatic emphasis and a drolly rolled *R*, I wasn't sure whether he had said "*La Rrrouille!*" (Rrrust!) or "*L'Art--ouille!*" which would translate as: "Ouch! Art."

Talon was an artist. While every Sunday he would go to the Atlantic coast and paint watercolor marines, his true genius lay in sanding and painting houses. My waning interest in rust was rekindled later when another Henri, my great-uncle, came to visit from Paris. Henri Rabaté, an engineer who had graduated from the prestigious École Polytechnique, was a world-renowned expert in paints. He was a formidable man and a reputed wine expert who had a knack of, with just a twist of his fingers, producing shiny coins from my ears, nose, or hair. I didn't know then that Uncle Henri had authored an encyclopedia and a trilingual dictionary of paints and solvents. As Monsieur Talon was an amateur painter, Uncle Henri was an amateur poet, a born raconteur who loved telling tall tales. His magnum opus was published the year I was born: a trilingual glossary in French, English, and German, delineating all the industrial elements needed to make waxes, oils, resins, pigments, varnishes, inks, paints, and even household cleaning products.[1] He had calculated the exact amounts of pain protecting the Eiffel Tower and had finished an Eiffel Tour assignment.

He would quiz me: how much does all the paint covering the famous Tower weigh? I learned the correct answer: sixty tons! Such an unimaginable amount—an ocean of liquid!—impressed me no end. Uncle Henri explained that the Tower constantly had to be repainted and its myriad light bulbs changed regularly. The Tower has been repainted eighteen times since its completion in 1889. Old Parisians know that the Eiffel Tower has changed its color more than once. A few might remember its red-brown hue turn to yellow-ochre, as one can see in a famous sequence of Louis Malle's *Zazie dans le métro*.

Today, the Tower is a lovely metallic bronze that somehow mimics the innumerable tin replicas made in China for tourists. Its color dissolves at the top with a neatly engineered optical illusion; its color remains uniform when viewed from the ground. What most visitors are not told is that the original metal elements of the Tower have all been replaced over time. The Eiffel Tower mirrors the Ship of Theseus, the age-old thought experiment about whether the replacement of all of the ship's parts renders it an entirely different ship, or if it, in essence, remains the same. In this case, the ancient paradox finds rationale in rust, and in the fact the Eiffel Tower was originally meant to stay in place for only twenty years. At first, the locals hated it. Within twenty years, the

Tower had become such a symbol of Paris, and by extension of the whole of France, that it could not simply be taken apart—it had to be repainted.

When the time for a new coat of paint returns, twenty-five painters toil on the structure with harnesses and bosun's chairs in a feat of acrobatic redecoration lasting a whole year. Uncle Henri had a brother who was a minor poet, a translator of Serbian epic poems. His 1926 collection of poems, *Sillages et Sillons*, included a sonnet about the Eiffel Tower at sunset that I had memorized; alas, I now only remember the final lines. The sonnet ends with a gloriously kitschy metaphor presenting the Tower as a sledge-hammer flattening the setting, a gold-ingot sun on an enormous anvil coming out of the fire god Vulcan's forge. Even in 1926, one could not avoid technological similes when waxing lyrical in front of the Tower. My great-uncles could have quoted Shakespeare's Sonnet 65:

O, how shall summer's honey breath hold out
Against the wrackful siege of batt'ring days,
When rocks impregnable are not so stout,
Nor gates of steel so strong, but time decays?

What is true of the Eiffel Tower is true of most postindustrial places. Let me recount another personal anecdote. In my early teens, my younger brother and I used to meet with friends from the neighborhood to play soccer. A favorite activity on the weekends was sailing on small boats in the quiet waters of Bassin d'Arcachon, a triangular bay open to the ocean. A member of our group had a father who was a radiologist and owned several boats, including a superb racing yacht. During winter, we would accompany him to the dry dock up on the estuary where he checked that his boats were properly sanded, caulked, and repainted. I discovered the magnitude of the bigger boats' rusted hulls, scraped by entire groups of workers; I was awed by the size of container ships and cargo freighters kept dry. Our immersion in that culture, so foreign to our city lives, led to the idea of calling our boys' club the "Club of the Rusts" (*le Club des Rouilles*). As the initiator, I proclaimed myself "The Human Rust"; the others, four or five in all, chose nicknames involving rust. We would call each other "rusts" as we bobbed on the waves in our small skiffs. The image that triggered our zany idea—those dry docks in which upside-down hulls were scraped by workers—was our first glimpse of what Camus was calling a "Sisyphean myth." Floating on tiny wooden planks, we were forced to consider the clash between wood and iron. We imbued it with a metaphysical sense of wonder, worrying less about how metal structures weighing tons could be floating than about a weird choice of materials constantly attacked and corroded, oxidized by water, salt, and air. Having chosen rust as our totem, we strived to acquire some of its underhand, stealthy power.

Paint provided an answer to rust that was less metaphysical. Much later, I discovered that one of my favorite authors, Ettore Schmitz (who signed his books Italo

Svevo), was an expert in maritime paints. Svevo had married his rich and beautiful cousin Livia Veneziani, whose father's company manufactured industrial paints for the Austrian navy. Svevo became a partner in his father-in-law's thriving business in 1897. At heart, he was an artist, a modernist whose two published two novels, *Una Vità*, in 1892, and *Senilità*, in 1898, suffered the same fate: dismal sales and negative reviews. Svevo proved to be more successful in his commercial activities. His letters to his charming wife allow us to follow him as he travels from Trieste to London in June 1901.[2] Svevo works for a while in Chatham where he performs paint trials for the Royal Admiralty's naval dockyards, just to test the Veneziani underwater paint. He proves to the British Admiralty that his paint is the best in the world: the Veneziani paint would keep His Majesty's warships free of rust and corrosion permanently. The paint was adopted by the entire British fleet. In order to consolidate the fantastic contract, Svevo opened a branch in London. Thanks to his efforts, the Veneziani company became the exclusive paint supplier of the world's largest navy. Meanwhile, trying to give up smoking and complaining of his poor English, he missed home. His British stay was marred by silly linguistic misunderstandings.[3] Back in Trieste in 1907, he enlisted the services of an Irish expatriate by the name of James Joyce—a meeting that had momentous consequences for the literature of modernism.

More recently, I found an equivalent of the awe and thrill I experienced before rusting ship hulls when discovering a breathtaking installation entitled "Temp'L." The South Korean group Shinslab had displayed it between July and October 2016 in the plaza of the Museum of Contemporary Art in Seoul. The architecture firm had recycled parts of an old French liner and fitted the inside space with trees, plants, and benches. The old ship had been sliced off at one end and turned upside down, providing a public resting space, the huge metal structure creating a beautiful pavilion in the entrance courtyard of the National Museum of Contemporary Art.

The old ship's external surfaces had been left raw and scratched while the inside was painted in glossy white paint. Within was the steel lattice that supported the body of the steamer and newly added spiral staircases and balcony.[4] It felt as if an enormous whale had been gutted and turned inside-out and upside down. You were greeted by the scarred and bleeding flesh of the animal, while the smooth coating of white paint evoked the protective skin of a welcoming, homely, almost bourgeois interior.

Shinslab had chosen a French boat for this Korean installation. The reason given in the notes was Le Corbusier. Indeed, one sheet reproduced Le Corbusier's modernist illustration in his 1923 *Towards a New Architecture*. Le Corbusier superimposes the Cunard liner "*Aquitania*" and iconic Paris buildings, Notre Dame, the Tour Saint Jacques, the Arc de Triomphe, and the Opera. Side by side, the ancient monuments are smaller than the mammoth liner. Le Corbusier wanted to "compare" traditional buildings with modern icons of technological prowess.[5] He had been extolling the technological sublime that he found in liners, airplanes, silos, and industrial buildings. In the same 1923 book, other icons of modernity include the terminal elevators in Canada or North America. These same structures, today, are all being destroyed by wrecking balls. For Le Corbusier they marked a standard of modern beauty—today, they are examples of our "deindustrial sublime."[6] By cutting and inverting the oxidized prow of the old liner, Shinslab Architecture points to the closure of a modernist utopia. Rust invading the surface of the hull testifies to the corrosion of the modernist dream of purity.

The spread of rust on metal surfaces is most prevalent and visible in the northeast of the United States. I was pleased to be hired by the University of Pennsylvania in the 1990s—this gave me an excellent opportunity to observe rust firsthand. Every day brought its treats. As for rust, I have never been disappointed by Philadelphia, Pennsylvania. A simple bus ride from Center City to North Philly provides countless views of abandoned warehouses, sagging bridges, unused oil cisterns, decaying steel mills, broken down factories turned into crack houses, unused industrial machinery from the 1920s emerging between collapsing walls—not to speak of old ovens, refrigerators, and battered heaters that dot the sidewalks under the elevated subway in the area called Kensington. A cab ride to the airport reveals the intertwining of cisterns new and old, so rusty that they seem ready to explode, and recycling facilities where corroded old cars are compacted and stacked. A train ride to New York offers more postindustrial delights. Metal poles twisted, corrugated iron sheets, oxidation seeping under sturdy concrete underpasses, rust is everywhere. Only on reaching the glittering façades of Manhattan can one forget it.

I still wonder why rust is more on display in North America than in Europe or Japan.[7] Are Europeans or Japanese so ashamed of rust that they cover it up quickly and paint it in gaudy colors? Nevertheless, rust is more prevalent in the United States, and its associated costs are much higher than in Europe. The US Federal Highway Administration in 2002 released the study "Corrosion Costs and Preventive Strategies in the United States" on the prevention of metallic corrosion in the US industry. In 1998, the annual direct cost of corrosion in the United States had been 276 billion dollars, 3 percent of the gross domestic product—a small improvement from 1995, when the cost of corrosion nationwide had amounted to 300 billion dollars per year.

Today, in the United States, rust causes countless bridge accidents and car malfunctions. In 1983, rust caused the collapse of the Mianus River Bridge near Greenwich, Connecticut. The bridge's neglected bearings had rusted internally, slowly pushing one corner of the road slab off its support. Three drivers died when the slab collapsed into the river. In 1967, rust caused the Silver Bridge disaster in West Virginia: the steel suspension bridge collapsed, killing the forty-six drivers and passengers on the bridge. Recent books like Jonathan Waldman's *Rust: The Longest War*[8] recount many incidents of that type, while other books like Allen Dieterich-Ward's *Beyond Rust*[9] examine how cities like Pittsburgh have managed to overcome the rust belt syndrome. My first chapter will look at films and books that stage rust as a danger by testifying to the end of technological optimism. I will roam between the rust belts of China, Australia, and Pennsylvania to try and see modern rust as a global phenomenon, after which I will link what appears as a pure historical factor to a phenomenology of the human body—for, as we know but tend to forget, the fact is that our blood is red because of the presence of rusting iron in its hemoglobin. These apparently irreconcilable images will begin to merge in the works of writers as diverse as Hegel, Ruskin, Coetzee, Kafka, and Hugo von Hofmannsthal.

1 HOW TO LIVE WITH GLOBAL RUST

What is rust actually? The technical term for rust is "corrosion," a slow form of burning that affects the surface of metals before modifying its texture. The corroded layer changes its color and functions as protection from external interference for a while until it thickens and cracks. The flaking allows for more moisture to penetrate until the cycle is repeated and the corrosion reaches deeper. The end result is the transformation of iron and steel into compounds like iron oxide. Indeed, another name for rust is "oxidation," referring to the chemical process yielding a film of iron oxide (FeO, Fe_2O_3, or other derived oxides) on the metal.[1] The formula for iron oxidation is the following:

$$Fe + \tfrac{1}{2}\,O_2 + \tfrac{1}{2}\,H_2O \rightarrow Fe(OH)_2$$

Followed by:

$$2Fe(OH)_2 + \tfrac{1}{2}\,O_2 + H_2O \rightarrow Fe(OH)_3$$

Fe(OH)$_3$ or hydrated ferric oxide is the main form under which rust is known. It is insoluble in water and recognizable by its typically reddish-brown color. Fe(OH)$_3$ should not be confused with Iron(III) oxide or ferric oxide (Fe$_2$O$_3$). Iron(III) oxide is an inorganic compound, one of the three main oxides of iron, next to Iron(II)oxide or (FeO), and Iron(II, III)oxide or (Fe$_3$O$_4$). As a mineral, ferric oxide is known as hematite, a main source of iron for the steel industry. Fe$_2$O$_3$ is dark red and readily attacked by acids. Often, one calls "rust" Iron(III)oxide, as both have a similar structure.

As most car owners learn sooner or later, a deep scratch made on any part of the vehicle will present traces of corrosion in a matter of weeks if not days, depending of course on the weather, on the presence of humidity or, worse, of salty water. People tend to believe that only iron can rust, trusting that "stainless steel" will remain rust-free. In fact, any type of steel will rust. However, there is some hope: repairs follow a simple enough pattern, sanding the spot, priming, and painting. Ready to start again!

One realizes quickly that time is built into the dialectical interaction of metal and rust. How long will my scratched car look good without a fresh layer of paint? Should I repair my rusty secondhand car or just buy a new one? Is it safe to jog beneath several rusty, crumbling bridges along the Schuylkill River Trail? Automobile makers, like those from other metal-reliant industries, see rust not just as an enemy against which more efficient protection technologies have to be invented, but also as a tricky ally: rust increases the obsolescence rate of machines with iron components. Goods, machines, engines will have to be discarded, destroyed, and replaced—a boon for an economy of abundance, an economy in which objects are regularly discarded and new ones bought. In economies of scarcity, as in certain African villages, local industries hinge around the repairing, cleaning, and recycling of parts or wholes. *Wounded Objects: Repairs in Africa*, a wonderful exhibition organized by Gaetano Speranza at the Musée du quai Branly in Paris in the summer of 2007, explored the amazing ingenuity displayed by local populations, ranging from the Maghreb to Gabon to Dogon territories, in the repairing of old objects. Ancient techniques like sewing, hammering, nailing, screwing, welding, and soldering were and are still used in creative and poetic fashions. "Rust," then, is partly a subjective factor; recycling has no end, from direct work on the objects themselves, to the way ancient iron production would reuse parts of the material. Moreover, since rust and its attendant processes end up dissolving old metal components, one can argue that rust serves an ecological function, a point to which I will return in the last chapter.

"Rust" is also the name of a color. Iron(III) oxide is used for different types of pigment like "Pigment Brown 6," "Pigment Brown 7," and "Pigment Red 101." Pigment Red 101 is an important inorganic colorant characterized by opacity, tinting strength, dispersibility, light fastness, and weather resistance. It is used in concrete, roofing tile, stucco, masonry, paint, coating, rubber, plastic, paper, and leather industries. Umber is a natural brown or reddish-brown earth pigment containing iron oxide and manganese oxide. It is slightly darker than the common earth pigments ochre and sienna. The color "burnt umber" is produced by heating umber clay, so as to dehydrate iron oxides. They turn into red hematite, commonly used for paint.

In another domain, rust is a disease of the plants caused by pathogenic fungi. There are almost two hundred rust genera producing more than seven thousand species of rather scary vegetal parasites. Rust affects otherwise healthy plants, infecting the leaves, tender shoots, stems, and fruits. Plants that are infected appear stunted, crippled, yellowed, or discolored. The name of rust was given by analogy, because most of the times the effect of the parasite is to create a yellow-orangey powder. It lands on vegetation and produces pustules that form on the lower surfaces; it can potentially devastate large-scale agriculture. To give one example, in the nineteenth century, the British-controlled Ceylon (Sri Lanka today) had been producing huge quantities of coffee. By the late 1860s, a coffee leaf rust fungus ominously called *hemileia vastatrix* reached the island.

Ceylon had some 160,000 hectares in coffee plantations. Because the planters had no fungicide at their disposal, the fungus spread until nearly all the trees were defoliated. Ceylon had been exporting about a hundred million pounds of coffee a year but, by 1889, production was down to five million pounds. In twenty years, most coffee plantations were wiped out. Ceylonese coffee production all but ceased, which led to the replacement of dead coffee trees with tea bushes. By chance, no fungus invaded the tea crop at the time, and soon after fungicides were synthesized to protect tea bushes. In order to escape the rust disease, coffee production moved to Brazil, Colombia, and Central America, where it still dominates today.

We will return to the biological associations of "rust" not only in its semantic closeness to vegetative rot, but also in the way contemporary artists like Gal Weinstein have made productive use of the link between metal rust and vegetal rust. However, when we talk about "rust," plants are not our first thought. In our mental associations, "rust" evokes our "Rust Belts," those bygone centers of industrial manufacturing, much more than teeming parasites devastating plantations. For most, rust is a visible symptom of postindustrial societies. This aspect looms in the imagination, and I will study its representations in recent films and novels.

1 Rust Belt stories

Most Rust Belt stories, fictional or not, documentary or romanticized, begin in the same way: an exposition about how many jobs have been lost since the factories closed. When we open Paul Hertneky's touching memoir *Rust Belt Boy: Stories of a An American Childhood*, we learn that

Eastern Pennsylvania steel industries lost 300,000 jobs in a very short time, the exodus starting in the late 1970s:

> Ironically, roughly six million African Americans fled into the north when the industrial revolution began, and the same number of industrial workers moved out when the era ended a hundred years later. But the Great Migration north took fifty years to unfold, whereas the emptying of the Rust Belt took place in only twenty years.[2]

Hertneky, a steelworker himself whose family originally came from Slovakia, states that the local interdependence of steel and immigrants from all nationalities and backgrounds lent resilience despite terrible loss: "Like tempered steel, the locals have been made sharper and stronger through extreme stress."[3] This concept of resilience after mass disaster is a trope of Rust Belt stories.

One of Hertneky's anecdotes comes from a childhood marked by the smell and feel of metal:

> Our lives were filled with discarded molten material—ash used for traction in the snow, nuggets of pig iron, sharp metal sheets, iron fillings we gathered with magnets, mercury we kept as a treasured plaything, pipes welded together for the batting cage and plates walling our steel dugouts, corrugated sheets we learned to cut and bend into sleds and shields. . . . Like all boys, I was drawn to the ways it rusted and flaked when I rubbed it, the way

it rang against a ball-peen hammer, the way it smelled, sometimes pungent enough to make my fillings hurt.[4]

In the chapter "Rust and Restlessness," he reminisces about his and a friend's ill-concocted scheme. They wanted to make pocket money by convincing a rich neighbor, Tierney, that his rusty metal fence needed to be repainted. Tierney, taking them at their word, asked for an estimate. They measured the fence and asked for $300 to wire-brush, prime, and repaint the metal. The offer was accepted on the spot. Then they realized that they had underestimated the task: the brushing and scraping of iron curlicues and filigrees became an endless and thankless chore. No sooner had they peeled away the rust in one part than they had to cover it in thick lead-based paint, lest the rust set in again. After two months of hard toil, the boys realized they had worked for a measly sixty-two cents per hour. However, this was still welcome sum of money; first, the pride of knowing that, to this day, the old fence has not rusted. Then Hertneky's friend made good use of the lesson by becoming, like my uncle, an expert in paints, solvents, and resins. As for Hertneky, the experience led him to write, for, as he says, rust leads to narratives: "And I have come to see rust as a weathered narrative, blistered by time and neglect, shedding tales of Vulcan's men, calling upon the restless to apply a durable sheen."[5]

A similar evocation of an industrial catastrophe provides the backdrop for an ambitious first novel by Philipp Meyer, *American Rust*. It is set in Buell, an imaginary rust belt city in the Monongahela Valley, some forty miles south of

Pittsburgh, Pennsylvania, a place where the steel mills closed in 1987. Isaac English, small and brainy, and Billy Poe, an athlete and a hunter, are on the cusp of adulthood. Isaac, tired of living with his depressed father, a retired widower, steals all the money in the house to run away to California. He enlists the help of his school buddy Poe, who, although reluctant to leave, accompanies him partway. They find shelter from the rain in an abandoned factory, where three scary drifters arrive to claim the place as theirs. Isaac turns to leave when threatened, but Poe is stuck behind. Hearing him scream inside, Isaac selects a weapon from a heap of rusty metal: "Underneath the other scrap—he reached his hand carefully through the stack of rusted metal to where a dozen or so industrial ball bearings were scattered in the dirt. He picked one up. It was the size of a baseball, or larger, cold and very heavy."[6] He comes back to see Poe almost stabbed, and hurls the ball bearing at one of the three men, killing him. This absurd murder renders any dream of escape impossible. Part of the plot revolves around the fact that Poe is suspected, not Isaac. Poe ends up in jail, where he is almost killed; Isaac turns himself in, but the friendly cop (who shot one of the drifters himself) does not press charges. Before being caught, Poe goes hunting, trusting the Valley to help him recover soon (p. 97). This novel leaves open the allegorical meanings of its title. The act of violence that destroys the plans for a future life of the two heroes is presented as a combination of the dark industrial past, a continuous menace, and the signs of renewal from within the realm of rust itself.

I want to shift to a different setting, moving from the American rust belt to Australia. In *The Fine Color of Rust*, a 2012 novel by P. A. O'Reilly, the power of rust over individuals is also presented as an unavoidable fate, but in a different key. The main character, Loretta Boskovic, is a mother of two who has been abandoned by her husband. Her husband ran away after ten years of marriage, leaving her with minimal resources to bring up two children in Gunapan, an imagined small town near Melbourne. Loretta is losing her looks as she struggles to care for a difficult eleven-year-old daughter who misses her father and a clingy, affectionate six-year-old son. We follow her in hot inland Australia, through landscapes of dusty farms, junkyards, malls, and diners. The plot begins when Loretta decides to fight against the government's plan to shut down Gunapan's only school. Loretta tirelessly rallies the local community, pleading their cause so well that the education minister of the country visits the town. The minister agrees to let the school stay for two more years. But then Loretta and her close friend, the old junk man Norm, discover more problems in their small city, where political corruption is rife. Thus, the city council tries to get Norm's blight of a junk heap removed in order to start a Leisure Resort Area that will benefit local investors with unacknowledged ties to the politicians.

Here, the junkyard provides a multiple allegory. It is repeatedly described as a "spectacular landmark, mounds of glowing red rust, the metal mountain of the south"[7] in which Norm lays out in the open "tractor parts, rolls of wire, mowers, corrugated iron sheets all rusted and folded, bits of cars and engines, pots and pans, gas bottles, tools, toys, bed frames, oil drums, the chipped blades of threshers and harvesters."[8] At first, the junkyard appears as a sign of industrial decay and impotence. The decay is mitigated by the return of Norm's estranged son, Justin, from a twenty-year jail sentence. We learn later that Norm had been battling his advanced skin cancer all the while. He soon dies, to Loretta's deep chagrin. The death of her closest friend sends her into a frenzy of activity and even acting out—she slaps the rich woman who is going to benefit from the resort and enlists more help from new friends who are instrumental in helping her denounce their shady schemes.

We also see Loretta's husband come back with a young sexy woman in tow—the novel does not provide an easy solution to all the plotlines whose outcomes look like failure after failure. When the daughter reconciles with her dad, Loretta discovers, to her shame, that her brash children have been harassing and abusing children of a family recently arrived from Bosnia. Loretta faces the deep mold of intolerance growing in her own backyard, as it were. At another level, industrial rust parallels Norm's lethal skin cancer. A surprise comes at the end: in fact, Norm had made a lot of money by gambling on horses. His derelict junkyard was less a sign of his inability to sell his old rusty machines than an act of artistic creation. The objects he had accumulated spell "S. O. S." when seen from the sky, creating "a new image made from junk."[9] Rust offers an ambiguous image—resilience accompanies the ability to see beauty in small things. Hence the epigraph, to which I will return: "The Japanese have a word, *sabi*, which connotes the simple beauty of worn and imperfect things: a weathered fence; an old crackling bough in a tree; a silver bowl mottled with tarnish; the fine color of rust."[10] The Japanese concept conveys an aesthetic lesson (one should be ready to see beauty in apparent imperfection) and an ethical lesson: such imperfection, once fully understood, can give you more courage to face family worries and overcome political adversity. Rust is thus not a burden or a blemish but a mode of expression combining ethics and aesthetics.

2 Rust and trust

Making a tiny jump from Japan to Manchuria in Northern China, I will now discuss *Rust*, a Chinese documentary greeted with great acclaim when it was released in 2002. *Rust* is the first part of an epic triptych totaling nine hours, a surprisingly engrossing and lyrical unanimist hymn to rust. The film was shot in the city of Shenyang, in the district of Tie Xi Qu, in which an enormous industrial complex had been built during the Japanese occupation in 1934. The Soviet Union expanded it further in the 1950s; the expansion reached a climax in the mid-1980s. More than a million workers were employed there before 1990. At that juncture, China converted to a market economy and the old industries closed, one by one. From

December 1999 to April 2001, Director Wang Bing went there to film the slow death of these factories, the entirety of the trilogy *Tie Xi Qu: West of the Tracks*.

In the first part, *Rust*, the gigantic industrial halls appear like a Dantean hell. Heat generated by the activities contrasts with the snow and bitter cold of the weather. We follow workers who have less and less work to do. Their role has shrunk to almost nothing, the specter of unemployment closing in. One shouts to the filmmaker: "Film that place, soon nothing will remain!" The documentary presents as an epic of loss, obsolescence, and hopelessness, but its particular technique suggests something else.

We are treated to very long sequences, beginning with a slow train ride through Shenyang, the urban landscape soporific as it is blanketed in snow. Wang films the showers, the common rooms, the interstitial spaces where workers relax, play mah-jongg, sip tea, fight, laugh, insult, and chat endlessly. Armed with a rented digital video camera held against his chest, Wang captures all the details of everyday life of the workers who remain in these crumbling factories. He makes us perceive different shades of red in the rusting machines, we almost feel the steam released by the workers' baths and the toxic fumes that they inhale without using the recommended protective masks, out of sheer ignorance. The immense industrial complex appears as a dying monster that has not completely destroyed the workers' simple joys: eating, drinking tea, playing at games, but, above all, waiting, worrying, and hoping.

In a groundbreaking essay, Manuel Ramos-Martinez discusses the links between the film's technique and its main theme, rust.[11] Refusing to treat the film as an example of "objective" documentary that would present reality as such, Ramos-Martinez argues that the film's technique is defined by the phenomenon of rust:

> But it is not social ruins that play the leading role in *West of the Tracks*, rather the pervasive phenomenon of oxidation. What the film lays bare is rust, that is to say, a permanent anticipation of the ruin. And this, above all, with a view to showing its fundamentally intrusive power: rust in the factory walls, in the machinery, in the train tracks, in the households. Moreover, rust is not a simple motif, but it impregnates every take of the film.[12]

Ramos-Martinez implies that rust colors the film to the point that our own vision becomes rusty as a consequence.

In his analysis, a sense of "oxidation" alludes to the way Wang baffles and subverts our expectations. Ramos-Martinez claims that the long tracking sequences of the film "oxidise the standard function of recording the ephemeral."[13] The idea is that the film is not a detached documentary, but a heavily participatory first-person narrative. Indeed, the filmmaker is not transparent, for he becomes a witness who consents to immersing himself "in the rhythms of the factory, in its invitations and interruptions."[14] In *West of the Tracks*, Wang's body is discreetly present: we hear footsteps, we see its shadow at the frame's edge. Once in a while, a worker will talk to Wang who mumbles a short reply. Holding his mini-camera against his chest, Wang cannot help recording minute bodily movements when he explores the huge steel mills, blast furnaces, smelting facilities, and plating plants.

The second implication of the idea of the "oxidation" posited by the film is political:

> The political significance of *West of the Tracks* does not simply lie in the representation of the workers left behind by the transformations of the Chinese socio-economic landscape, but rather in the oxidation (which is something other than a simple break) of this social function and its associated epistemic positions, as they pertain to the film-maker, the spectator and the social actors.[15]

Ramos-Martinez alludes to declarations made by Wang, who denied having any political program to defend, reaffirmed that he did not have any filming strategy.

Ramos-Martinez assumes that this quasi-improvised quality of the filming process dismantles the usual protocols of sociological interpretation. The concept of an oxidized gaze would directly challenge the possible identification of the spectator with both the camera's gaze and any presumed social function of the characters seen on the screen:

> The rust of the camera's gaze makes it difficult for spectators to focus on and simply identify with the place

of address or with the social actors. The workers appear in these long, long takes not so much as social actors but as nameless ghosts wandering around the space in question.[16]

The process would destroy any empathy, any position of mastery, and furthermore any production of knowledge. Instead of knowledge and mastery, there would be distance, estrangement, and dislocation. At the end of the film, according to Ramos-Martinez, we would know less about the factory than at the beginning because, through its relentless "oxidation," the film would have demonstrated the impossibility of fathoming what happens there.

Can we follow this analysis in terms of a "rusty eye"? What does the suggestion of a "corrosion of perception" actually refer to? We might understand this analysis in the context of an ontology of the image, a concept launched by Roland Barthes with *Camera Lucida* in 1981, and expanded by Kaja Silverman in *The Miracle of Analogy*.[17] Silverman's subtle analysis of nineteenth-century photographs argues that photography teaches us to see analogically. Silverman contends that photography develops *in* us by a process of analogical transfer. Can we push the idea to argue that Wang's long takes teach us to see "rustily"? There would be a deliberate contamination of our gazes by the obsessive theme of rust shown in all its manifestations.

Innovative and intelligent as it is, the concept of an "oxidized gaze" does not do justice to the film's declared strategies and ambitions. In an interview with the *New Left Review* in 2013, Wang remained closer to a simple denunciation of the nefarious sociological changes brought about by the introduction of a neo-capitalist system in China:

> This is the changing China. Factories of the past still had a collective spirit. Workers' lives were related to the factories. For instance, if you were a formal worker here, you would be considered part of the ownership of the workplace. Likewise, people's daily life was closely related to their work relation at the factory. That is no longer the case for production units today—now there is a contract-labour system everywhere. . . . The workplace is no longer intrinsically related to your life.[18]

In order to nuance what might sound like a blunt statement, I will quote another interview, this time given by Wang to Jérémie Couston for the French weekly *Télérama*. Couston asked Wang who, according to him, might be an "absolute artist."[19] Immediately, Wang replied "Joseph Beuys" and recounted Beuys's famous performance *I Like America and America Likes Me*. The German artist was wrapped in felt in Düsseldorf, driven to the airport in an ambulance, flown to New York, taken to a gallery where he was locked in a cage for three days with a coyote, and then whisked back to Germany.

The film *Rust* is situated between these two extremes: on the one hand, it testifies to a changing social reality by taking factories themselves as the main, dynamic characters of the film, not the workers whom we see more or less idle; on the other hand, it shows the body of the artist in his genial but offhand distance from the workers' plight. Like Beuys, Wang works with his own body whose interactions with the world are both staged and directly experienced. His aim is to analyze, explore, and represent the resilience of human beings. The keyword is thus resilience more than resistance, for, as Wang stated in the same interview, he had absolutely no wish to "change the world."

In two excellent essays on Wang's film *The Nameless Man* from 2011, the art theorist Georges Didi-Huberman[20] begins by rejecting the knee-jerk "criticism" of films. Even though he acknowledges the temptation to produce "critique" himself, he feels more inclined to "follow" Wang in his peregrinations; that is, to go where his gaze goes. Wang would thus give us a wonderful lesson in "materialist history" but would redouble it as a lesson in "humility."[21] On this reading, Wang would usher in a poetics of poverty and mute survival encompassing the absurdity of pure life and the material conditions of production. A new style of thinking would be warranted by Wang's work: the critical attitude must change by opening itself to terms like "confidence" or "trust." To think about "trust" instead of "rust" entails that one will suspend a critique of the "system's ills" and instead engage in criticism of oneself as an autonomous subject who sees, feels, and knows an object. Watching Wang's work requires then that we unlearn our usual modes of viewing not just by "oxidizing our vision," which suggests a simple contamination, but by finding the courage to trust Wang's vision. Such a trust would mean unconditionally saying "Yes" to what one sees. If we are brought closer to trust than to rust, one issue remains: the ability to treat it not as a simple symptom of industrial decadence, but as potential for a subjective transformation. This simple reversal will be exemplified by Coetzee's novel *Life & Times of Michael K*, to which I will turn soon.

In fact, Wang may not have imagined when he shot his film that, by 2007, the factory area of Tie Xi would have been turned into a series of residential zones. The unrest of the turn of the century has almost been forgotten. One important historical detail about Tie Xi is not mentioned by Wang: in 2000, the industrial workers who had been laid off started a series of demonstrations, blocking the roads in the city and region, and repeating their protests more than a hundred times in one year.[22] However, thanks to new investments and new directions, the "Tie Xi syndrome" was soon over. Soon, the old factories were turned into museums of industrial production. By 2011, only three large industrial enterprises remained in the Tie Xi district, functioning as "live museums" of the past. The specialized industrial parks are very popular today, and one can visit a "Modern Architectural Industrial Park," a "Casting and Forging Industrial Park," and other similar iterations.[23] What rendered this retrospective gaze possible was the development of modern tertiary industries and the establishment of new city centers where the old plants had been; Tie Xi was reborn through the revitalization of the old industrial zone.

3 Rusting the Age of Iron, or dialectics at a standstill

To understand rust better, one should immerse oneself in it, thus becoming rust, as it were. This is an idea that has been treated imaginatively by J. M. Coetzee in *Life & Times of Michael K*. With Michael K, Coetzee invented one of his most endearing and frustrating characters. He is a black, hare-lipped gardener who manages to weave his way to paradoxical freedom in a fictional civil war coming at the close of the Apartheid period in South Africa. K is defined by his stubborn refusal to conform to any social or political model. The story begins when he accomplishes his dying mother's wish to be buried in the Karoo farm where she was born. After she dies on the way, he continues the pilgrimage alone, carrying her ashes with him. After many tribulations, he arrives at a farm that may be the one his mother's wished. There, K grows pumpkins, oblivious to the realities of the civil war. The grandson of the farm owners is a white deserter who flees from the ongoing civil war and hides in the premises. K refuses to be his servant; also he avoids taking sides in the raging conflict, because for him the only thing that matters is to grow vegetables, pumpkins particularly. As Coetzee explained, the book's plot took a life of its own: "It didn't turn out to be a book about becoming . . . but a book about being, which merely entailed that K go on being himself, despite everything."[24]

I will focus on one moment when the hero achieves pastoral bliss and enjoys the peace of an unencumbered idleness—significantly, the main image is that of rusting iron:

> He could lie all afternoon with his eyes open, staring at the corrugations in the roof-iron and the tracings of rust; his mind would not wander, he would see nothing but the iron, the lines would not transform themselves into pattern or fantasy; he was himself, lying in his own house, the rust was merely rust, all that was moving was time, bearing him onward in its flow.[25]

This paean to rusty idleness evokes the only freedom K experiences: he can work at his own rhythm, which entails sleeping a lot and not eating very much. K nevertheless needs a water pump to create favorable conditions for pumpkin growing. He is not a luddite, but rather dreams of being a "parasite" on the land. Like Wang's "nameless man," who sleeps in a little hole he has made in the ground,[26] Michael K also becomes a sort of mole burrowing in the soil.

Coetzee suggests that by staring at the rusting iron and becoming one with matter and time, K enacts the semantic echo sending us from "rust" to "rustication." Here is "rustication" with a vengeance, a masticated rustication one might say—if one can follow the progress of rust on iron rust, rust and organic growth exchange their properties.

Before this discovery, K was a meat-eater. In a nightmarish scene, K corners and drowns a wild goat in a dam. He cuts it up and cooks a haunch and eats the flesh, but then feels feverish. He buries the remains of the goat and decides not to kill large animals. He limits himself to small birds that he shoots with a catapult. Then, he decides to be fully and only a "gardener":

> His deepest pleasure came at sunset when he turned open the cock at the dam wall and watched the stream of water run down its channels to soak the earth, turning it from fawn to deep brown. It is because I am a gardener, he thought, because that is my nature.[27]

He starts planting seeds in the earth where he had spread his mother's ashes. But then he is caught by the police and sent to a relocation (read: concentration) camp. After his escape, K goes back to the farm and resumes his activities, careful not to betray his presence, not even to the rebels who arrive and occupy the premises. He sees the fruit of his labor grow, comparing the melons to "sisters" and the pumpkins to "brothers."[28] He eats the first of his pumpkins, relishing the deep orange flesh, at last tasting "perfection."[29] It is the first time in his life that he eats something with pleasure. It is at this juncture that he gazes at rusty corrugated iron. The color of rust is a visual parallel of the color of the pumpkins. A curious period begins, when he only eats his own "children," whether melons or pumpkins, and feels a curious "taste of blood in his mouth."[30] But then, he slips into a dreamy, anorexic stupor and almost starves to death—until he is found by the army and assumed to be a rebel.

Brought to a second camp, he is treated less as a dissident than as a sick man by a kind medical officer, aghast at seeing the human skeleton K has become. The officer nevertheless fails to ask K what he would like to eat, and is surprised to see that K starts eating when he is given grilled pumpkin. Trying to explain that he is "not in the war"[31] and is only a gardener, K launches into the most explicit explanation of his position: he states that the vegetables he was growing on the farm did not belong to him but to the earth: "What grows is for all of us. We are the children of the earth."[32] The officer misunderstands this remark because he associates K's veneration of the earth with his devotion to his dead mother and hence to death itself. He is quite wrong, as the rest of the novel teaches us.

K's political passivity has been understood as referring to Gandhi's movement of passive resistance, a movement he launched in South Africa before the First World War to protect Indian immigrants. However, Gandhi believed in a good "cause" and in the power of his exemplary gesture to promote a just struggle, whereas K has no political beliefs at all. When he tells the medical officer that he and all men are the children of the earth, his statement alludes—without his being aware of it, of course—to Plato's concept of the "noble lie." In the *Republic*, Socrates wants to persuade the future citizens of the ideal state that differences in status were justified by the "nature" of each person, shaped and created by the earth:

And when they were quite finished the earth as being their mother delivered them, and now as if their land were their mother and their nurse they ought to take thought for her and defend her against any attack and regard the other citizens as their brothers and children of the selfsame earth.[33]

The myth of "autochthony" transforms citizenship into a family but naturalizes the differences between subjects, whose souls will be identified by a type of metal: gold for the philosophers and rulers, silver for the soldiers and administrators, iron for the artisans and farmers. No one will rebel against a social status handed down from before birth by the earth. Marc Shell has commented on national myths that transform the affairs of the political community into a blood community. Shell points out that the theories of universal fraternity end up justifying incest.[34] If Plato's myth of autochthony defines all subjects as born from the earth, the earth replaces human mothers. Plato's fiction remains a "beautiful, necessary lie." This lie would be justified if it forced everyone to accept a given social status as stemming from Nature. Then no worker, no peasant, no humble servant will try to ascend beyond a lowly station.

We can understand why K has to become "rust"—here is a sign of his disinclination to obey laws that "are made of iron" (p. 151). The iron lie participates in the essentialist lie that ascribes to K his lowly "iron" nature. Coetzee went on to publish *Age of Iron* in 1990, a novel in which the indictment of the Apartheid followed a pathological trajectory: the nice old lady, a retired Classics professor dying of cancer, signifies that the white liberal minority cannot do much to change the situation, in spite of well-meaning efforts. In 1983, when writing *Life & Times of Michael K*, Coetzee attacked the Apartheid laws—laws made of iron—once more. Thus Noël, the older medical officer, confides to his younger colleague: "'You need an iron man to run an iron camp. I am not that kind of man.' . . .'I could not disagree. Not being iron is his greatest virtue.'"[35] By contrast, K's perfect pumpkins prove that rust can bloom and produce fruit. By a reverse magic, when he waters his iron "essence," it oxidizes and turns into edible products like savory pumpkins. His treasure, after his mother's ashes that have spawned and multiplied as so many children of the earth, little brothers and sisters, is a bag of pumpkin seeds. The myth that K perpetuates is that of children that can be planted as seed, gathered as crops, and then devoured. The myth should allow for an organic, vegetable, unstoppable metamorphosis of rust. Here is edible rust, at last; it points to the "green rust" that we will discover at the end of this book. If this metamorphic and organic rust entails rustication, it is not via a regressive and lethal return to the mother's womb, as the medical officer mistakenly believes, but as the consequence of a rigorous meditation on the dialectics of images that underpin our trust in progress, if such a trust is a condition for history to be meaningful.

Here is the aspect that had shocked a colleague of Coetzee, a committed South African writer who thought that they were comrades-in-arms and fighting against the horrors of the Apartheid. When she read *Life & Times*, Nadine Gordimer reacted with pained surprise. In a scathing review that attacked the political quietism of the main character, she noted that all of the novel's characters seem to be equally fatalistic:

> Yet the unique and controversial aspect of this work is that while it is implicitly and highly political, Coetzee's heroes are those who ignore history, not make it. . . . No one in this novel has any sense of taking part in determining that course; no one is shown to believe he knows what that course should be. The sense is of the ultimate malaise: of destruction.[36]

If Gordimer has a point, her reading suggests that Coetzee's novel offers us a Benjaminian allegory, an allegory underpinned by pure destruction, as what he perceived in Baudelaire's poetry. Walter Benjamin insisted on the artificiality of the modern allegory that presents itself as a nonorganic ruin: "Allegory holds fast to the ruins."[37] Allegory proceeds from a destructive furor and dispels the illusion that all proceeds from an organic wholeness. In a spirited discussion of Benjamin's *Arcades Project*, Coetzee notes that allegory replaces abstract thought and theory for Benjamin. He concludes his review in a somewhat critical or disabused manner: "The Arcades book, whatever our verdict on it—ruin, failure, impossible project—suggests a new way of writing about a civilization, using its rubbish as materials rather than its artworks: history from below rather than from above."[38] This seems to define very well K's perspective on history.

From such a discussion, which could be infinite, we might try to derive a lesson, a rusty lesson that Walter Benjamin could have heeded especially when he criticized the belief in progress. Benjamin, perhaps because he endorsed Giedion's modernist faith in the steel structure of arcades,[39] never seems to question the positive role of iron in modernist construction. In fact, Benjamin appears almost too "constructivist" when composing the great unfinished urban poem of his *Paris Arcades*. Benjamin never pays attention to the fact that the Paris arcades that he takes as his main trope were also rusting, that they were more than outmoded, literally insalubrious, and full of human and animal excrement—at least if we follow the evocation provided by Louis-Ferdinand Céline, who knew them well having spent his childhood in one of the them, Passage Choiseul (ironically rebaptized "Passage des Bérésinas," in an allusion to the Napoleonic defeat during the campaign of Russia). Benjamin, who had read Céline's *Journey to the End of the Night*, seems not to have known this. It is nevertheless worth being reminded of this other side of the iron-and-glass structure that so impressed the Surrealists and Benjamin. Whereas Benjamin marveled at the fact that the Paris arcades were interior and exterior spaces at once, the doctor diagnoses in Céline's sarcastic autobiographical novel, *Death on the Installment Plan*: "Your Passage is . . . a urinal without door or windows."[40] Another vignette is as scathing:

> I have to admit that the Passage was an unbelievable pesthole. It was made to kill you off, slowly but surely, what with the little mongrel's urine, the shit, the sputum, the leaky gas pipes. The stink was worse than the inside of a prison. . . . The Passage took cognizance of its asphyxiating stench. . . . We talked of nothing but the country, hills and valleys, the wonders of nature.[41]

This time, rust would be the material symptom of a general disease, an urban consumption calling up the demise of the petty bourgeoisie, the disenfranchised Parisian *Lumpenproleteriat* tempted by fascism, as Céline would soon be.

When history cannot go forward, when its dialectics remain at a standstill, the danger is that an "age of iron" will then just rust. Let it rust and then explode, this would be the hope that Benjamin derived, not without misgivings, from surrealism. For Benjamin, the main discovery of surrealism was the effort to enlist the "energies of intoxication" for the revolution to come. If he took Louis Aragon's novel about the Paris arcades, *Paris Peasant*, as a literary model, the method had been invented by André Breton, who had made an astonishing discovery:

[Breton] was the first to perceive the revolutionary energies that appear in the "outmoded"—in the first iron constructions, the first factory buildings, the earliest photos, objects that have begun to be extinct, grand pianos, the dresses of five years ago, fashionable restaurants when the vogue has begun to ebb from them. No one can have a more exact concept of the relation of these things to the revolution than these authors.[42]

Breton and Nadja together "bring the powerful forces of 'atmosphere' (*Stimmung*) concealed in those things to the point of explosion."[43] Rust is not just a floating signifier because it can function as a Benjaminian allegory, whose model is Giotto's Charity as presented by Proust and to which we will soon return. With Giotto, we discover a rusticated Charity trampling on all metals, whether base or noble, to assert equally the grace of God and the bounty of nature.

2 HEGEL AND RUSKIN: DIALECTICS OF THE ORGANIC AND INORGANIC

1 Hegel and the restlessness of rust

If we wish to avoid a rusty (or rust*ing*) "dialectics at a standstill," we need to combine a dialectics of history with a dialectics of nature, as Hegel did. The issue of iron and rust in the *Philosophy of Nature* begins in a discussion of the differences between metals: noble metals like gold, silver, and platinum are contrasted to less precious metals like iron. Precious metals appear purer—they are less corruptible and evince a lower "readiness to form oxides."[1] These metals do not oxidize when exposed to heat or air; the rationale of their stability is enduring self-identity. Solidity and noble purity are interpreted as a "lack of difference."[2] Gold is the apex of rare metals: "The Notion of this solid, simple nature of metals seems to be represented in its purest form by gold; that is why gold does not rust and old gold coins are still untarnished.[3]" By contrast, lead and iron, followed by metalloids and unstable alloys, are subjected to the vagaries of oxidation—of rust—via exposure to air and water.

How many precious metals are there altogether? Three, four? Schelling wanted to include mercury in the group, but Hegel refuses:

> Those metals are not to be regarded as precious in which form is most separated out of indifference with the essence, and in which selfhood or individuality is the predominant feature, as in *iron:* nor are those metals precious in which the incompleteness of form vitiates the essence, making them impure and bad, like lead, etc.[4]

The distinguishing feature of iron is that iron is not stable enough to be identical with itself. This is why its pliancy and its ductility enable the active dissolution called rust.

The discussion of precious or semiprecious metals helps Hegel make sense of the phenomenon of electricity, or "Galvanism,"[5] soon introduced because, according to Hegel, iron would be a better conductor of electricity than gold (we know today that this is not the case). What stands out is Hegel's understanding that the difference between metals is mediated by electricity and water. This view entails that oxidation—rust—plays a key role:

Through the neutrality of water, and hence of its real capacity for differentiation . . . a real (not merely electrical) activity develops between the metal in its state of tension and the water; with this, there is a transition from the *electrical* to the *chemical* process. Its production is oxidation generally, and deoxidation or hydrogenation of the metal (if the process goes so far), or at least the generation of hydrogen gas and likewise oxygen gas: that is, a positing in the abstract, independent existence (§ 328) of the differences into which the neutral Element has been sundered; just as, at the same time, their union with the base comes into existence in the *oxide* (or *hydrate*): the *second* kind of corporeality.[6]

We now understand better the problem posed by iron's individuality and its attendant lack of gravity. Iron is prone to dissociation in a corrosive process that weakens and separates its elements. Its substance will be split up by reduction until it merges with one of the four elements: nitrogen, oxygen, hydrogen, or carbon.[7] In that list, oxygen stands out as the main "consuming element."[8] Hegel argues that the process of disintegration is to follow a rigorously logical nature:

The chemical process is therefore a *syllogism*; and not merely the beginning of the process but its entire course is syllogistic. For the process requires three terms, namely, two self-subsistent extremes, and one middle term in which their determinatenesses come into contact and they are differentiated.[9]

The example taken here is lead: lead soon loses luster and sheen in pure air but this luster endures if lead is plunged in a glass of water. This process applies to rust: "The same is true of iron: rust, consequently, is formed only when the air is moist; if the air is dry and warm, the iron is not affected."[10] In the end, the process generates "a totality returning to itself" as a consequence of "a circle of *particular processes*."[11] What Hegel is stating in this abstract language is that Nature functions like a huge body in which dissociation is not a negative end-term but a relay on the way to further productions and reproductions.

As Markus Semm has observed,[12] for Hegel the deployment of the Spirit in Nature—an unfolding that guarantees the syllogistic form of the exchanges upon which rust is predicated—takes the shape of a general rhythm: it marks the tempo of a vital pulse. Nature develops its totality in as much a biological as a musical manner. Its rhythmic exchanges are grounded on a pulsation that runs through all phenomena. The most salient example is given by the blood coursing through all living bodies. Here, Hegel finds another proof of the relevance of his natural dialectics:

This dissolution of this persistence is the pulmonary system, the true, ideal process with the outer world of inorganic Nature, with the element of air; it is the organism's own self-movement which, as elasticity, draws air and expels it. The blood is the result, the organism which through its own interior process returns into itself, the living individuality which makes members (*Glieder*) into viscera. The blood as axially rotating, self-pursuing movement, this absolute interior vibration, is the individual life of the whole in which there is no distinction—animal time.[13]

Following this, Hegel describes the formation of blood with a mixture of concrete and abstract elements:

The blood elaborates itself from the air, the lymph, and the digestion, and is the transformation of these three moments. From the air, it takes pure dissolution, the light of the air, oxygen; from the lymph, the neutral fluid; from digestion, the moments of singularity, the substantial moment. And as thus the whole individuality, the blood opposes itself to itself afresh and generates shape.[14]

Hegel needs two more pages to develop all the details of these three successive transformations. Blood defines the individuality of the living subject, but its general pulsation follows a universal law. Blood embodies or allegorizes the work of the Concept: "The endless process of division and this suppression of division which leads to another division, all this is the immediate expression of the Notion (*Begriff*) which is, so to speak, here visible to the eye."[15]

One key factor has to be added to this rhythm of negation and *Aufhebung*—it is the "irritability" of blood:

Blood in general, as the universal substance of every part, is the irritable concentration of everything into the interior unity: it is heat, this transformation of cohesion and specific gravity—but not merely the dissolution produced by heat but the real, animal dissolution of everything. Just as all food is converted into blood, so, too, blood is dispensed as the source from which everything takes its nutriment. That is what pulsation (*Pulsieren*) is in complete reality. It has been said that the juices, because they are secreted (*das Ausgeschiedene*) are inorganic and that life belongs solely to the solid parts. But in the first place, such distinctions are in themselves meaningless, and secondly, blood is—not life, but the living subject as such, in opposition to the genus, the universal.[16]

Thus, in the end, the global picture drawn by Hegel is that of a vital life circle constituting a perpetuum mobile.[17]

For Hegel, blood, not the heart, is the main agent of the dynamic process. The heart is just a muscle that pumps, it is a material cause, whereas blood allegorizes vital dynamism itself: "This is the blood, the subject, which no less than the will initiates a movement. As the whole movement, the blood is the ground and the movement itself."[18] As Hegel states, the movement of blood is its own absolute law, which is why, as he adds, an invalid who remains immobile too long develops ankylosis.[19] Hegel follows this example with a discussion of the difference between arterial blood, redder, because it contains more oxygen, and venous blood, bluer, because it contains less.

A later section devoted to breathing tackles the cause of such an endless movement by deploying a term that Hegel adopts from writings of Albrecht von Haller, the concept of "irritability." Blood is fundamentally "irritable." Evoking doctrines that reduce the workings of the heart to its response to mechanical forces, Hegel then comments rather critically:

> But all these mechanical explanations of the physiologists are inadequate. From whence comes this elastic pressure of the walls and the heart? "From the irritation (*Reiz*) of the blood" they reply. According to this, therefore, the heart moves the blood, and the movement of the blood is, in turn, what moves the heart. But this is a circle, a *perpetuum mobile*, which would necessarily at once come to standstill because the forces are in equilibrium. But, on the contrary, this is precisely why the blood must be regarded as itself the principle of the movement; it is the "leaping point" (*punctum saliens*), in virtue of which the contraction of the arteries coincides with the relaxation of the ventricles of the heart.[20]

Indeed, William Harvey, who had discovered the circulation of the blood in the body, described the heart of the embryo as a *punctum saliens*. This tiny, pulsating point is the first spot at which the heart perceptibly beats. Refusing to proclaim the heart as the prerequisite for blood circulation or vice-versa—a classic chicken-and-egg scenario—Hegel posits the "self-movement of blood" as the true agent of the organic life cycle. If blood can become a "subject," it is because its "will" initiates the whole movement.[21] Here is one rare moment when Hegel seems to anticipate his future enemy, Schopenhauer; however Schopenhauer's "will" is unconscious and a-subjective.

Francis Glisson had introduced the notion of "irritability" as early as 1650, when he tried to determine the causes of ailments like rickets. In *De Natura Substantiae Energetica* (1672), Glisson developed the idea of a natural energy flowing throughout the body—a blind energy he called "irritability" capable of being transformed into sensation. The "irritable" reaction of organs like the intestines or the heart generates excitement, which leads to specific actions and more general bodily functions. Glisson's idea goes beyond a mechanical application of a stimulus; he presupposes a physiology of the living dynamism that he called *biousia*. This autonomous substance of bodies and organs reacts to all stimuli without thought, consciousness, or actual sensation.

Nearly one century later, the Swiss physician Albrecht von Haller embraced this concept in his 1752 "Dissertation on the Sensible and Irritable Parts of Animals." Attempting to regulate the dangerously materialist suggestion that there might be something like a blind will, animated and persisting autonomously in all living substances, Haller had to differentiate between sensation and irritability. Thus, sensation would belong to nerves, irritability to muscles. When Haller discussed the link between blood and the heart, he restricted the application of irritability to cardiac muscle—in his view, the heart is "irritated" by an influx of blood, to which it responds with its familiar contractions.

In a passage that almost ends the *Philosophy of Nature*, Hegel goes further than Haller—as we have seen, he accuses Haller of falling into a chicken-and-egg trap. In fact, Hegel returns to Glisson's *biousia* when he presents irritability as more than a *Reiz*. Irritability, for Haller, means "response"; he uses *Reizleitung* to mean "conduction of impulses," while suggesting "appeal," "charm," "attraction," "excitement," and "stimulation." For Hegel, irritability is the very principle of subjectivity; it is an endless negativity at first functional in blood before turning into thirst, hunger, and desire. Hegel explains this idea some ten pages later, when discussing animal instinct and respiration: "The respiratory process is a spontaneously interrupted continuity. Exhalation and inhalation is a volatilization (*Verdunsten*) of the blood, the volatizing irritability (*verdunste Irritabilität*)."[22] Here, because the mechanism of the lungs seems parallel to that of the heart, Hegel returns to his previous analysis of blood:

Now why is the blood connected with this ideal assimilation of the abstract Element? The blood is this absolute thirst (*absolute Durst*), its unrest (*Unruhe*) within itself and against itself; the blood craves to be ignited (*hat Hunger nach Befeuerung*), to be differentiated. More exactly, this assimilation is at the same time a mediated process with air, namely a conversion of air into carbon dioxide and venous (dark, carbonated) blood, and into arterial, oxygenated blood.[23]

This analysis leads to a magnificently lyrical evocation of blood as a living process that perpetually consumes itself: "Air is in itself the fiery and negative element; the blood is the same thing, but as a developed unrest—the burning fire of the animal's organism which not only consumes itself but also preserves itself as fluid and finds in air its *pabulum vitae*."[24] Here, we see at work this "restlessness of the negative" that Jean-Luc Nancy has identified as Hegel's main conceptual discovery.[25] Blood therefore allegorizes subjective negativity, albeit concretely and in bodily terms; we remember that rusting iron would herald a similar negativity by slipping its inner dissolution into the old vitalism inherited from Glisson. Such a restlessness—one is tempted to call it "rustlessness"—is not, for all that, ruthless. The restlessness of rust follows a law, the law of life whose regeneration presupposes endless division and recombination. Hegel did not have at his disposal the conceptual hinge that would have made his dialectics more persuasively teleological: the knowledge of the fact that blood is red because of the oxidized iron—the very process of rust—it contains. It remained to a later thinker to make the connection explicit; this was John Ruskin's task, but to perform it he had to appeal to a different dialectical movement.

2 Ruskin: Nothing blushes like rust

"The Work of Iron, in Nature, Art and Policy," the text I will now focus on is from a lecture given in February 1858, at Tunbridge Wells. Ruskin, already well-known as an authority on Italian art and a critic-patron of the modernist painter J. M. W. Turner, chose a most homely topic for this affluent audience: he would give a speech on rusty iron. The lecture was included in the 1859 collection *The Two Paths*, public lectures outlining Ruskin's views on art and society in an easy and accessible manner. For him, art was always a means for an end or, rather, end*s*. These ends included a better life, a better economy, a just management of the world. When addressing the public of Tunbridge Wells, Ruskin began by stating his personal connection with the place, a famous resort known for the quality of its springs and its mineral-rich waters. Discussing iron in general, Ruskin is in fact gesturing toward the source of Tunbridge Wells's fortune—iron was the backbone of "present prosperity of the town."[26]

Since prehistoric times—the Iron Age, at least—people mined the iron-rich rocks in the Tunbridge Wells area. Early in the seventeenth century, Lord North persuaded King James I that the springs had had a miraculous influence on his health, which then turned the city into a spa retreat. One century later, Beau Nash became the fashionable master of ceremonies for the court and the rich families gathering there. The town remained a popular resort and was still thriving when Ruskin lectured. He had often visited spas as a child, for his health had been delicate. Ruskin explains that he keeps delectable memories of wandering the countryside in search of spring water welling from marble basins over an "orange rim," or clear water sparkling over a "saffron stain,"[27] all obvious traces of iron deposits on stone.

This image segues into the first discussion: "Iron in Nature," where Ruskin develops the familiar association between iron, water, and rust:

You all probably know that the ochreous stain, which, perhaps, is often thought to spoil the basin of your spring, is iron in a state of rust: and when you see rusty iron in other places you generally think, not only that it spoils the places it stains, but that it is spoiled itself—that rusty iron is spoiled iron.

For most of our uses it generally is so; and because we cannot use a rusty knife or razor so well as a polished one, we suppose it to be a great defect in iron that it is subject to rust. But not at all. On the contrary, the most perfect and useful state of it is that ochreous stain; and therefore it is endowed with so ready a disposition to get itself into that state. It is not a fault in the iron, but a virtue, to be so fond of getting rusted, for in that condition it fulfils its most important function in the universe, and most kindly duties to mankind. Nay, in a certain sense, and almost a literal one, we may say that iron rusted is Living; but when pure or polished, Dead.[28]

In line with Hegel's theoretical rewriting of vitalist philosophy, Ruskin develops the idea that oxygen provides the breath of life to iron, as it does for animals and humans. Iron is similarly animated when it breathes that elixir of life just by getting rusty. There is a fundamental difference, however, between animal life and metal life: a metal cannot excrete what it absorbs: "The metal absolutely keeps what it has once received of this aerial gift; and the ochreous dust which we so much despise is, in fact, just so much nobler than pure iron, in so far as it is *iron and the air*."[29] The service rendered by this compound is the ability to return all of its elements to the earth, "in making the ground we feed from, and nearly all the substances first needful to our existence. For these are nothing but metals and oxygen."[30] By a reversal of Hegel's point of departure, the most precious metal, gold— which shall not even be named—is the culprit of all social evils: "There is only one metal which does not rust readily; and that, in its influence on Man hitherto, has caused Death rather than Life; it will not be put to its right use till it is made a pavement of, and so trodden under foot."[31]

The old trope of a capital city like London with its streets paved with gold—an ancient Biblical image, too—clashes with the pastoral simplicity of a place like Tunbridge Wells. Ruskin knows that it is another metal, steel, that would develop gold's lethal propensities. He conjures up a vision of desolation, if the earth "instead of its green and glowing sphere, rich with forest and flower, showed nothing but the image of the vast furnace of a ghastly engine—a globe of black, lifeless, excoriated metal?"[32] Against this apocalyptic future (or past), one must champion a worldview predicated on human reciprocity and natural exchange. It is in this context that rust will be seen to breathe: "Softening from its merciless hardness, it falls into fruitful and beneficent dust; gathering itself again into the earths from which we feed, and the stones with which we build—into the rocks that frame the mountains, and the sands that bind the sea."[33] The beautiful evocation of a dynamic Nature in which the earth replenishes itself and offers its bounty to its inhabitants leads to a reconsideration of the apparently ignoble function played by rust.

Rust is not only visible proof that metals can decompose into natural elements, it also supplies a central feature of the soil: the color of landscapes. Ruskin argues that without the presence of iron, the earth would be white, moreover "not pure white, but dirty white."[34] Gravel in flower beds would turn the color of ashes. Pathways in country walks would be gray soot. And ploughed fields, instead of displaying "deep folds of a mantle of russet velvet" would turn into "gristly furrows in a field of mud."[35] Even the sands by the seas would look like a drab slime. Here is the refrain: "That is what it would be without iron."[36] While Ruskin doubtless exaggerates the impact of iron on the color of the earth, it is quite true that well-drained soils will be richer in oxygen, and appear red and brown due to the oxidation of minerals containing iron. Lack of iron oxide in soil yields a gray pallor, and Ruskin concludes triumphantly: "Iron is in some sort, therefore, the sunshine and light of landscape, so far as that light depends upon the ground."[37]

There is another source of light and life to be found in iron, and it is most visible in buildings. Ruskin contrasts the homely, comfortable appearance of English villages with the villages he has seen in his trips abroad, mostly in Switzerland, Scotland, and Italy. They may be more picturesque, but they lack the specific British quality that he identifies with the use of bricks and tiles: "The greater part of that warm and satisfactory appearance depends upon the rich scarlet colour of the bricks and tiles."[38] This reddish hue is "warm" for Ruskin, evoking an old woman dressed in a red cloak. And the color of the tiles is not produced by paint, but by nature—the clay used in England is naturally red (due, of course to its iron content). This is what prevents cottage roofs from looking like "unbaked clay, the color of street gutters in rainy weather."[39]

Particularly praised are the Welsh slates used to cover roofs in the villages of the region; their hues are of "warm purple" kind due to a complex mixture of vermilion, gray, and violet: "Whatever brightness or power there is in the hue is entirely owing to the oxide of iron."[40] In a vast reconstruction of the composition of the earth, Ruskin distinguishes three types of soil: clay, lime, and flint, the main substances that Nature works with. Like an artist, Nature varies its effects endlessly. Ruskin offers many examples; I will quote what he writes about marble:

All those beautiful violet veinings and variegations of the marbles of Sicily and Spain, the glowing orange and amber colours of those of Siena, the deep russet of the Rosso antico, and the blood-colour of all the precious jaspers that enrich the temples of Italy; and, finally, all the lovely transitions of tint in the pebbles of Scotland and the Rhine, which form, though not the most precious, by far the most interesting portion of our modern jewellers' work;—all these are painted by Nature with this one material only, variously proportioned and applied—the oxide of iron that stains your Tunbridge springs.[41]

Here again, Ruskin inflates the role of iron in his reconstruction—indeed, if iron oxide causes yellow and brown deposits in the limestone, iron and manganese usually generate pink and red colorations.

Ruskin's twentieth-century disciple, Adrian Stokes, had a more scientific approach when he adduced his own observations of the geology of building stones. In *Stones of Rimini*, Stokes defines marble as "metamorphosed limestone."[42] In an extraordinary paean to limestone,[43] Stokes finds Ruskinian accents and rhythms when he stresses the link between the soft stone and the local environment: limestone is presented as a link between the organic and the inorganic. Stokes develops the idea that limestone, like marble, is by nature a condensation of the past. With limestone, the past is visible in its very materiality:

The adjustment between lime and rain by which rain is conserved in the rock so often at the expense of lime in the soil, calls for the adjustments that man will make. . .. Lime keeps soil neutral, prevents it from growing acid or sour, and consequently infertile. It also prevents alkaline conditions and promotes oxidization of the organic material.[44]

Stokes does not dwell on the idea of oxidization, but his general drift includes the process of rust in the evolution of "organic materials" like lime. Such interactions all make us see in geographical and atmospheric conditions the traces of a connection with a longer past. Indeed, limestone, marble, and rust present slices of frozen and petrified time:

Limestone, for the most part formed of organic deposits, is the link between the organic and the inorganic worlds. Limestone exhibits in mummified state the life no longer found of the Silurian and other distant ages, just as the Istrian palaces of Venice present to us in terms of space, the hoard of ancient Venetian enterprise. The very substance of limestone suggests concreted Time, suggests that purely spatial or objective world which limestone architecture has organized for us.[45]

Thus, when Stokes takes us to Rimini or to Venice, he shows us not only the past of the Italian renaissance, but a more archaic conglomeration of fossilized forms of life. Then, according to him, one's unconscious will respond when sensing a resonance in this hidden past: "A Greek temple is an ideal quarry reconstructed on the hill. The Tempio Malatestiano at Rimini is an ideal quarry whose original organic substances were renewed by the hand of the carver to express the abundant sea collected into solid stone."[46] The carver's art externalizes the hidden life glimpsed in the stone. It endows it with a measure of immortality.

There is nevertheless a point that Adrian Stokes, even in his most private fantasies, did not dare to make. Stokes did not connect the material history of limestone and the bodies of both the people who crafted and the people who enjoyed the spectacle of those temples and palaces. Ruskin would do this, which is where his genius is apparent. Continuing his discussion of the mixture of clay, stone, marble, and limestone found in the British countryside, Ruskin concludes that these are ideally suited to the fair complexion of the British people:

A nobler colour than all these—the noblest colour ever seen on this earth—one which belongs to a strength greater than that of the Egyptian granite, and to a beauty greater than that of the sunset or the rose—is still mysteriously connected with the presence of this dark iron. I believe it is not ascertained on what the crimson of blood actually depends; but the colour is connected, of course, with its vitality, and that vitality with the existence of iron as one of its substantial elements.

Is it not strange to find this stern and strong metal mingled so delicately in our human life that we cannot even blush without its help? Think of it, my fair and gentle hearers; how terrible the alternative—sometimes you have actually no choice but to be brazen-faced, or iron-faced![47]

Ruskin feigns uncertainty about the origin of the color of the blood; however, he had read enough scientific literature to know that hemoglobin is colored red because of oxidized iron. With an extraordinary conceptual leap, Ruskin then presents the iron in blood as contiguous with the iron in the landscape. To be "brazen-faced" thus evokes an impious disposition—those who can blush retain a native modesty. Fourteen years later, Darwin would conclude his final masterpiece, *The Expression of the Emotions in Man and Animals*, with a long discussion of blushing. Darwin found the phenomenon to be universal among humans, whatever their color of skin, but not among animals—and idiots: "Blushing is the most peculiar and the most human of all expressions."[48]

Having reached this metonymic expansion of the redness associated with iron, Ruskin feels the need to backtrack. He tackles a more material use of iron and talks about the metal in terms of its function more than in terms of pure aesthetics. One should assess the kind of material an artist will use: one cannot use marble for too fine traceries, nor take iron when one should have selected stone—"If, you carve in the marble what will break with a touch, or mould in the metal what a stain of rust or verdigris will spoil, it is your fault."[49] Surveying the uses of "iron in art," Ruskin finds this metal capable of specific types of expression. He affirms the advantages provided by this plasticity and compares several types of ironwork decorating the balconies he saw in Italy and Switzerland—he praises the ductility of the material capable of rendering the intricate intermeshing of foliage. Then, he makes a general statement about the connection between artwork and emotion: good craftsmanship is meaningful only if it is accompanied by the "work of the heart."[50] We are thus brought back to Hegel's heart, but by another route.

What the "heart" means here is the link between aesthetics and ethics, or rather, politics. The following section tackles the politics of iron by considering tools like ploughs (playing a positive role) and their opposite, fetters and swords. The recurrent theme in these impassioned pages is an appeal to human solidarity against capitalist exploitation. Analyzing candidly and uncompromisingly the nefarious effects of what he calls "stealing,"[51] Ruskin uncovers a true "torture" that ends up causing the untimely demise of the poor. The image of blood now changes its value because it signifies both the shame of the exploiters and the dire consequences of exploitation for the victims of speculation. Ruskin denounces a capitalist market rigged by banks that will not hesitate to ruin entire families: "And then consider whether the hand which has poured this poison into all the springs of life be one whit less guiltily red with human blood than that which literally pours the hemlock into the cup or guides the dagger to the heart?"[52] Pushing his rhetorical advantage, and quoting huge chunks from the Bible, Ruskin refuses to excuse anyone in his audience from such a knowledge: one cannot argue that no sin has been committed because such exploitation was "unconscious," for no one can remain in ignorance.[53] He adds: "There may be hope for the man who has slain his enemy in anger; hope even for the man who has betrayed his friend in fear; but what hope for him who trades in unregarded blood, and builds his fortune on unrepented treason?"[54] The denunciation may be shrill, but it is effective and unsparing. The blush of rusty iron has now infiltrated more than the landscape—the whole national "policy" is being indicted via the theme of blood. The red color of blood is not, however, only negative. Ruskin always hopes to reconcile his aesthetics with an ethics of justice to come—the utopia of the compassion and sympathy of a new heart.

In a letter dated July 1, 1871, Ruskin discusses the Paris Commune. He is appalled at the news that federate workers have set fire to the Louvre. Nevertheless, Ruskin expresses his solidarity with the workers' insurrection and calls himself a "Communist of the old school—reddest also of the red."[55] He opposes this strong color to the pink or "peach-blossom, dog-rose redness" of those who are half-heartedly on the left but hedge their bets. He belongs to the group of the "reddest of the red," and explains his meaning:

That is to say, full crimson, or even dark crimson, passing into that deep colour of the blood which made the Spaniards call it blue, instead of red, and which the Greeks call φοινικεος, being an intense phoenix of flamingo color.[56]

What distinguishes this group? They believe in giving above all, not in destroying art or the workers' tools. Their emblem is Giotto's famous "Charity," a woman who looks like a peasant and who—thanks to this very passage— impressed Proust so much.

In the *Swann's Way* volume of Proust's novel, we discover a kitchen maid working for the narrator's family in Combray. She has been identified by Swann, the aesthete, with Giotto's portrayal of Charity.[57] Giotto's *Caritas* is depicted as a peasant-looking woman in the "Allegories of Virtues and Vices" of the Scrovegni chapel in Padua. The narrator has a reproduction of this "Caritas" in his room (given to him by Swann) to ponder the way Giotto represented his Virtues as earthy, stolid, mannish, almost vulgar women. It will take some time before he can understand how modern allegories are material fragments of a whole whose symbolic meaning can be grafted onto the material body—in a word, the Benjaminian notion of allegories we have encountered earlier. Of course, Proust owed this insight to Ruskin. This is why, in his 1871 letter, Ruskin can present Giotto's Charity as a Communist of the deepest red, for with her feet, she "tramples upon bags of gold . . . gives only corn and flowers," while "God's angel gives *her,* not even these—but a Heart."[58]

3 INTERLUDE: BLOOD-WORK, RUST-WORK

When I was seven, a doctor examined my milky-pale, freckled complexion and concluded I was anemic. My fair skin was not common in the South of France; an ad hoc treatment was prescribed. In the afternoon, when I came back from school, a glass of fresh blood was being squeezed for me. Square chunks of raw horse meat were crushed in a grinder whose top screw made it look like a medieval torture device. A trickle of blood would fill a big tumbler. Every day, I choked down my glass of blood. The taste was sweet, with a metallic tinge that I ascribed to the metal of the machine. As a euphemism, the family designation was "meat juice." The surprising thing is that I did not turn into a vampire—or a vegetarian. Now that I think about it, I find the treatment less absurd, for even today, one finds websites advocating the regular consumption of fresh blood for anemic children.

In fact, both my parents and their doctor were laboring under a French delusion. They subscribed to what Roland Barthes has identified as a dominant French myth when analyzing *steak frites* (steak and fries) as a sign of typical Frenchness:

> Apparently steak's prestige relates it to its semi-rawness: blood is visible in it, natural, dense, compact, yet sectile. . . . Full-bloodedness is steak's raison d'être: the degrees to which it is cooked are expressed not in calorie units but in images of blood, rare steak is *saignant* when it is said to suggest the arterial blood of the animal whose throat has been cut, or *bleu,* which is the plethoric blood of the veins suggested by the purplish color, a superior degree of redness.[1]

Sadly, I was too young to drink wine; this would have been a solution had I been older. As Barthes notes in another of his "mythologies," in France, milk has always remained exotic, whereas wine appears as domestic.[2] Blood, then, was the-thing-itself, a way of communing with nature doubling as redemptive medication, that, even if it would not do the trick of curing, "couldn't hurt" me.

I learned later that there were worse blood diseases than anemia. Hemochromatosis, a primarily genetic condition that often afflicts Irish people, is characterized by an overload of iron in the blood. This iron invades vital organs like the liver, the heart, and the pancreas. Deposited in excess, iron poisons these organs; in a way, by rusting it rusts them. Its anarchic accumulation causes terrible damages like brain degeneration or even heart failure. One of the symptoms is a curious bronzing of the skin. The main remedy is the old medieval cure: bloodletting. All this derives from the fact that iron is potentially toxic when present in high quantities in the body.

The workings of blood, in what pertains to hemoglobin, are a riddle for most of us. The idea of "rusting" is not just an analogy. The iron contained in our hemoglobin does "rust," but in more complicated ways than any metal out there in the world. Ruskin had caught a crucial interaction when he perceived the presence of rusting iron in human blood. His intuition that iron in hemoglobin is what gives blood its red color was medically correct. There is oxidation of iron in the blood stream, even if the specific chemical bonds at work between iron and oxygen in blood are not identical with the bonds generating common rust.

Although the bond between iron and oxygen in hemoglobin is similar to common kinds of iron oxide in rust, hemoglobin commands a complex chemical structure entailing other bonds. In order for the iron and oxygen in hemoglobin to recompose into rust, the chemical bonds of the hemoglobin would have to first be broken. Hemoglobin contains heme groups, made up of big organic molecules with an $Fe(II)$ atom in the middle. The metallic iron is not "free," but already bound—that is, part of a compound. The iron, even if slightly oxidized, cannot react with oxygen freely as in rust because it is already bound to the nitrogen atoms of a bigger structure. Only under rare circumstances will one see the recomposition of rust occur: then the iron in hemoglobin can be further oxidized to ferric oxide or Fe(III) and reduced back to ferrous oxide or Fe(II).[3]

My so-called anemia was not such an exceptional circumstance. Usually, anemia generates a lowered capacity for the blood to carry oxygen, and one of its causes is iron deficiency. The lack of iron leads to a lack of oxygen—the chemical bond that allows oxygen to circulate is not able to form. Thus, the ingestion of blood cannot do much to change this vicious blood circuit, and belongs more to sympathetic magic. Horse-meat blood was supposedly less susceptible to parasites. My family being half-Belgian, this seemed natural—we would often eat *steak américain*, a Walloon delicacy, steak tartare mixed with a lot of mayonnaise and made of raw horse meat. By a nobly pious lie, I was told that the horses that offered their meat for my "meat juice" were very old horses, close to death, and that they did not suffer—a little myth worthy of the sentimentalism of the Victorian novel *Black Beauty*.

Was I, without being aware of it, included in a ring of "blood farms," like those still standing in Argentina and Uruguay? Blood farms rely on horses kept exclusively for blood extraction purposes. The blood drawn from the horses is then used by companies throughout the world that deal in medical research, diagnostic manufacturing, and veterinary drugs. A few years ago, traveling in the Jinan region of China, I discovered that the ancient medicine of *ē jiāo* (阿胶; 阿膠)

is still popular. This donkey gelatin is used as a "blood tonic." It is supposed to rebuild the body and compensate for blood deficiency, mostly for pregnant women or those with heavy periods. The collection of the gelatin involves more than the donkey hide, for fresh blood is needed for the final product. At least, it is mostly consumed in blocks of dried pieces, often melted down into a decoction of herbal mixture to drink. Nevertheless, the sad truth is that these donkeys have to be flayed alive.

As for me, for more than one year I was condemned to drink my horse blood on a daily basis, for my parents believed in its magic. Notwithstanding the pious lies about old horses being slaughtered out of mercy, I loathed the idea as well as the act of drinking this blood. I searched for a way of swaying my parents, whose motto was: "It's for your good." One day, an idea came to me. I began to run around in the garden, jumping around wildly, playing at being a horse, neighing like a colt, whinnying like a stallion. This was a time when my friends and I played Cowboys and Indians. Suddenly, I switched allegiances. I had been a Cowboy and all of sudden became of one of those Red Indians who owned barely tamed mustangs. My silly antics finally made an impression on my parents, to whom I had confided that I felt more and more like a horse. Fearing the onset of a psychosis more devastating than anemia, they relented and allowed me to sip less and less regularly of the bloody beverage.

My "becoming horse," as Deleuze would say, would soon be replaced, by a lateral sliding, with a metonymic displacement generating the later identification with "human rust." Indeed, "rust" and "Indian" shared a certain redness, and were coupled with a wish to win freedom. I had earned my freedom with a silly Indian ruse. What remains of my horse identification, which was something like the reverse of the Little Hans' phobia analyzed by Freud? It may have been the wish to rush at full speed that seizes me now and then, a wish best evoked by a short text Kafka published in 1912, in his first collection of short stories, "The Wish to Be a Red Indian."

> If one were only an Indian, instantly alert, and on a racing horse, leaning against the wind, kept on quivering jerkily over the quivering ground, until one shed one's spurs, for there needed no spurs, threw away the reins, for there needed no reins, and hardly saw that the land before one was smoothly shorn heath when horse's neck and head would already be gone.[4]

In order to prevent its metaphors from congealing, the text has to drink them or eat them as quickly as possible by going faster than its own images. Speed, the main feature of this fleeing body, will entail a surprising decapitation of the horse, which condenses the double logics of linguistic erasure and subjective withdrawal so prevalent in Kafka's stories. The vanishing horse evokes pure desire, the wish to move and be always elsewhere—its logic functions against that of later imagistic texts in which Kafka predicts his own death from tuberculosis, as in the richly evocative "The Vulture" from 1920. In "The Vulture," the narrator is in pain, relentlessly attacked by a vulture hacking at his feet. A passerby offers to help by shooting the nasty bird. The narrator agrees, but the animal anticipates its fate by hurling its body through the narrator's open mouth; it drowns in his blood: "Falling back, I was relieved to feel him drowning irretrievably in my blood, which was filling every depth, flooding every shore."[5] I will have to make a detour through Kafka's twisted metaphors in order to approach another side of rust in its essential connection with blood, but I will first evoke another animal.

4 IDIOMS OF RUST: RATS AND JACKALS, KAFKA AFTER HOFMANNSTHAL

When I was eight or nine, perhaps to make me forget my imaginary horses, I was given the very opposite of steed: a garden tortoise was my new pet. With a bold hypothesis on gender, I assumed that it was female and named her simply "Titine." Titine's domed back was dotted with lovely orangey squares, like a rusty three-dimensional chessboard. I composed a little ditty for her, a poem in rhyming slang: "*Titine, Rustine . . . Rustine, Titine!*" That song was my way of making her come out from her hiding place in the bushes; she would move along as fast as she could on her short legs, knowing that I brought delicacies, leaves of lettuce or parsley sprigs. In French, a "rustine" is a "repair patch" for a bicycle wheel or an inflatable boat; through this linguistic coupling, thanks to the little English I knew, *rustine* pronounced with a soft "R" made me associate Titine with rust.

Thus my tortoise would roam freely in our garden, the very embodiment of living rust in a pastoral setting. Alas, all pastorals soon meet an untimely end. Three years later, we came back home after a month spent at the seashore. Titine, left to her means in the garden with provisions, was nowhere to be found. The summer had been hot and dry. I was told that she had dug a tunnel under the wall and that she might come back. For a while, every evening I would circle the garden, singing my little song. In vain. I learned much later that Titine had died and was disappeared in secret. I was spared the pain via this pious lie, but for me, since that disappearance, I still hallucinate the rusty shine of an errant ghostly tortoise in distant gardens.

To make more sense of the specific vital and linguistic disappearance I associate with rust, I will discuss two texts that depict the process. Both enjoy an emblematic status in the literature of the German-speaking world. Each uniquely foregrounds the theme of rust, albeit with a different emphasis. I will look at Hugo von Hofmannsthal's 1902 *Letter of Lord Chandos* and then at Kafka's 1917 story, "Jackals and Arabs." They present a modernity predicated on a conceptual "rusting away" of any stable meaning.

1 The rust of words

In *The Letter*, von Hofmannsthal uses the mask of a fictional writer standing as his alter-ego. Philip Chandos, a British lord, sends a letter to Francis Bacon in 1603. Chandos explains to his illustrious friend why he has stopped writing. This account of an aesthetic and linguistic crisis mirrors what happened in von Hofmannsthal's career. He had been celebrated as a child prodigy for superb poetry published when he was sixteen. Three years later, the publication of two lyrical dramas, *The Death of Titian* (1892) and *The Fool and Death* (1893), was widely acclaimed. Von Hofmannsthal appeared as a promising representative of the Vienna "moderns," those aesthetes who followed the new vein opened by the symbolist poet Stefan George. Soon after, back from his military service, von Hofmannsthal experienced a writer's block but was able to transform it into a narrative.

The letter he published on October 18, 1902, in a Berlin daily, was a confessional manner of trying to make sense of a personal crisis. Like its author, Chandos confesses that he stopped writing because he has lost his trust in language: he no longer fathoms how words can describe the world. This letter is the inception of an awareness that a "crisis of language" occurs at the turn of the century, a crisis that defines the modern moment. Chandos probes the crisis further by showing that he has not only lost his grasp over language, but also his personality: the crisis of language doubles as a crisis of subjectivity. One of the images typifying the new disease, his sense of an estrangement between the world and words, is that of spreading rust: "Gradually, this contestation (*Anfechtung*) began spreading everywhere like an all-eating rust (*wie ein um sich fressender Rost*)."[1]

Hugo von Hofmannsthal's immersion in the works of Francis Bacon when writing his *Letter* in August 1902,[2] gave him the idea of using the name of the illustrious Chandos family (although no Philip Chandos is known). When his friend Leopold von Adrian objected to this antiquarian disguise, von Hofmannsthal replied that he needed the Elizabethan fiction to make a true confession.[3] Among the works of Francis Bacon, he had been struck by the "History of Life and Death." This compendium of observations on the duration of human and animal lives begins by surveying elements like metals. Bacon lists the properties of different metals, recalling Hegel: "Metals are of that long lasting, that men cannot trace the beginnings of them; and when they do decay, they decay through rust, not through perspiration into air; yet gold decays neither way."[4]

We know that von Hofmannsthal had read those pages; one *topos* developed by the fictional Chandos is mentioned several times by Bacon: the inconsolable sadness of the orator Crassus mourning the death of his favorite moray eel or *murena* (*eine Muräne*), a fish that lived to the age of sixty years. This anecdote is also found in Bacon's *Apophthegm* number 157 with a different moral twist.[5] Let us see how von Hofmannsthal presents his "case" to Francis Bacon. Philip

Chandos is twenty-six when he writes to Bacon. He begins by surveying his past achievements, his acclaimed poetic pastorals "reeling under the splendor of their word-plays."

> In all expressions of Nature I felt myself. When in my hunting lodge I drank the warm foaming milk which an unkempt wench had drained into a wooden pail from the udder of a beautiful gentle-eyed cow, the sensation was no different from that which I experienced when, seated on a bench built into the window of my study, my mind absorbed the sweet and foaming nourishment from a book.

The young poet felt that he was at the center of the universe; its signs, whether natural or cultural, he could decipher. A disease of his cognition leading to a quasi-mental collapse put an end to that dream: "My case, in short, is this: I have lost completely the ability to think or to speak of anything coherently."

The disease began when Chandos felt unable to use abstract words like Spirit, Soul, or Body. One day, as he was trying to explain to his four-year-old daughter that it was bad to lie, words failed him—his extreme linguistic dispossession forced him to act out, and he could only calm himself by galloping wildly on his horse. At such moments, his anguish functions as a negative force, an *Anfechtung*, a "contestation" and an inner contest or challenge, a moral dispute that attacks his mind when it spreads like rust. This verbal corrosion is not visible at first, for it attacks only the mind's voice. Soon, a dissolution of all the elements follow, which generates an altogether unstoppable splitting. It erodes the denotative link between words and referents that we take for granted. It spreads to anything that can be considered as a whole, splitting it in endlessly multiplying parts:

> For me everything disintegrated into parts, and those parts again into parts, allowing nothing to be encompassed by one idea. Single words floated round me; they congealed into eyes which stared at me and into which I am forced to stare back: this is a whirlpool that gives me vertigo and that, reeling incessantly, leads into the void. (translation modified)

Chandos tries to overcome the crisis by reading Seneca and Cicero, carefully avoiding Plato—the Latin authors' clear and ordered ideas should force him to think concretely and sequentially. However, if he can understand the words themselves, these texts stop making sense. Stymied, he decides to lead the mute, humdrum existence of other country squires, hunting on the grounds with friends, unencumbered by ideas. The text could end on this note of quiet despair—the lord's acceptance of his fate, his coming to terms with the fact that the life of the mind is now closed to him. However, at this point the text rebounds.

What makes von Hofmannsthal's affliction so modern is that the moment of utter dispossession reveals another way of perceiving the world, all the more intense as it remains beyond language:

> For it is, indeed, something entirely unnamed, even barely nameable which, at such moments, reveals itself to me, filling like a vessel any casual object of my daily surroundings with an overflowing flood of higher life. . . . A pitcher, a harrow abandoned in a field, a dog in the sun, a neglected cemetery, a cripple, a peasant's hut-all these can become the vessel of my revelation.

These "revelations"—one might call them "epiphanies," as Joyce did in 1902 and 1903, exactly during those years but in Dublin—occur outside language, in silent experiences of religious illumination. They generate moments of intense empathy. One crucial example given by Chandos is a moment when he identifies with a group of dying rats. He has ordered his servants to poison the rats infesting the milk vats in one of his dairy farms. He is not present while this happens, but riding peacefully on his horse as the sun sets down, he is suddenly invaded by the images of the scene experienced from the point of view of the rats, for, as he says, "all was in me":

> The vision of that cellar, resounding with the death-struggle of a mob of rats. I felt everything within me: the cool, musty air of the cellar filled with the sweet and pungent reek of poison, and the yelling of the death

cries breaking against the mouldering walls; the vain convulsions of those convoluted bodies as they tear about in confusion and despair; their frenzied search for escape, and the grimace of icy rage when a couple collide with one an-other at a blocked-up crevice. But why seek again for words which I have foresworn!

Comparing this experience with descriptions of panics in Livy, Chandos concludes that his immersion in the death throes of animals had

> something more divine, more bestial . . . it was the Present, the fullest, most exalted Present. There was a mother, surrounded by her young in their agony of death; but her gaze was cast neither toward the dying nor upon the merciless walls of stone, but into the void, or through the void into Infinity, accompanying this gaze with a gnashing of teeth! A slave struck with helpless terror standing near the petrifying Niobe must have experienced what I experienced when, within me, the soul of this animal bared its teeth to its monstrous fate.

This famous text was rewritten by Coetzee at the end of *Elizabeth Costello*. Costello, another fictional writer, argues that humans can feel what animals feel.[6] These animals are not just metaphors but imaginative bridges with a different mode of perception and consciousness. Chandos is quick to note that his empathy with the dying animals is not borne out of pity for the animals themselves, but out of raw identification. Similar experiences are triggered by the mere sight of a pitcher beneath a nut tree, or the vision of "a water strider skimming the surface of a lake from shore to shore." In those cases, a "combination of trifles" (*Zusammensetzung von Nichtigkeiten*) is enough to send through the young man "a shudder at the presence of the Infinite, a shudder running from the roots of my hair to the marrow of my heels" (translation modified). These "celestial shudders" are akin to "revelations," but they all beg for some form of language, a language as yet unavailable to Chandos. With a dialectical twist, he has recuperated his earlier ability to see a world full of being, only now the being shines forth in isolated parts rather than in unified wholes; its language of correspondences has been swallowed by muteness:

> It seems to me that everything that exists, that I can perceive, everything touched upon by my confused thoughts, everything has a being. Even my own heaviness, the general torpor of my brain, seems to acquire a being. I experience in and around me a blissful, never-ending interaction, and among the objects playing against one another there is not one into which I cannot flow. (translation modified)

Let us stress that Chandos can see *being*—but not *meaning*—around him. In a movement that announces what Rilke was to call "the Open," he wants to think through his body or through his heart, not through his words, so as to possess the mute exteriority of existence. Only by passing fully into a Lacanian Real exterior to any symbolization would one be immune to the rust of words.

After the first onslaughts of dispossession and alienation, a new calm takes hold of Chandos. The lord can occupy himself with the business of his estate, even while still desiring material ecstasies, seeking "among all the poor and clumsy objects of a peasant's life for the one whose insignificant form, whose unnoticed being, whose mute existence, can become the source of that mysterious, wordless, and boundless ecstasy." Minutiae are more likely to trigger these intense feelings than lofty or picturesque sights: his "unnamed blissful feeling is sooner brought about by a distant lonely shepherd's fire than by the vision of a starry sky." The young lord's unrest has not stopped, for he still hopes that he might find a new language sufficient for the experience. His letter ends with a premonition of a new language:

> The language in which I might be able not only to write but to think is neither Latin nor English, neither Italian nor Spanish, but a language none of whose words is known to me, a language in which inanimate things speak to me and for which I may, once in my tomb, justify myself before an unknown judge. (translation modified)

In the text, "rust" is one of the metaphors by which Chandos conveys the physical gnawing of subjective dissolution following the collapse of the correspondence of words and things. Language had first disintegrated like "moldy mushrooms" under the tongue. By the end, the metaphor becomes physiological; when the lord meditates on Crassus who, as we have seen, had fallen in love with his *murena*, the thought haunts his brain "like a splinter round which everything festers, throbs, and boils." The infection expands to the whole body and affects the very sense of subjectivity:

> I feel as though I myself were about to ferment, to effervesce, to foam and to sparkle. And the whole thing is a kind of feverish thinking, but thinking in a medium more immediate, more liquid, more glowing than words. It, too, forms whirlpools, but of a sort that do not seem to lead, as the whirlpools of language, into the abyss, but into myself and into the deepest womb of peace.

Hugo von Hofmannsthal was the first author who gave voice to the anxiety of a generation confronted with the excess of "things," an excess that would soon occupy Rilke and philosophers like Heidegger. Only a new language, yet to be invented, would be adequate to the task of giving voice to these mute ecstasies. Or, the old language would have to be scoured, cleansed, purified of its corrosive rust; this was the route chosen by the linguist Fritz Mauthner, then by the satirist Karl Krauss, both followed by Ludwig Wittgenstein.

However, to try and purify the language of democracy, to free it from the misdirection of vague slogans and empty words, was never Franz Kafka's aim. Kafka remained true to a modernist ethos; he was experimenting albeit without trying to invent a new language. His strategies were more devious and more humorous as well. This comes to the fore when we read his notorious allegory of the clash between Jews and Arabs in Palestine.

2 Kafka's rusty scissors

One of the most fascinating features of Kafka's "Jackals and Arabs" was that it was published in Martin Buber's Zionist review *Der Jude* in October 1917.[7] The monthly review started by Buber a year before, in the middle of the First World War, meant to serve as an open forum on issues related to cultural and political Zionism; a few of its editors were openly anti-Zionist. Altogether, Buber picked two of Kafka's stories. He chose "A Report to an Academy" for inclusion in a later issue. Kafka had written to him to explain that his stories should not be called "parables" but simply "animal stories."[8] Indeed, as if to confirm this insight, Kafka's reaction to the publication of the issue containing his stories was almost animal-like. He writes in his diary of October 1917:

> Orgy while reading the story in *Der Jude.* Like a squirrel in a cage. Bliss of moving, despair about confinement, madness in persistence, misery facing the immobility

outside. All this both simultaneously and alternately, even in the filth of the end.

A sunray of bliss.[9]

The expression of immediate joy leading to more ambivalent effects follows after another entry in the *Oktavheft*, an aphorism later collected among the Zürau series: "The true way is along a tight-rope, which is stretched aloft but just above the ground. It seems designed more to trip one than to be walked along."[10] Peter Sloterdijk has shown that the aphorism inverts Nietzsche's axiom from *Thus Spake Zarathustra* that "man is a rope over the abyss."[11]

From a tripping tightrope walker to a rodent running happily in its wheel, rotating everything except the frustrating stillness of the world around it—Kafka's intense joy would be generated by an animalistic movement, as strong as it is repetitive and absurd. This is the bliss that Kafka would experience when he felt that his writing had been successful, as he did after having penned "The Judgment." In those moments, his own writing could move him, and he would move along with its rhythm.

Kafka wrote this story between December 1916 and April 1917, just before the Balfour Declaration of November 2, 1917, the British pledge of supporting a Zionist state in Palestine. While no direct reference is made to that momentous decision, the discussions about the value of Zionism were heated in Prague at the time. One can say that the story condenses Kafka's conflicted relationship to Zionism and to his possible exile to Palestine. At first, the story's plot looks quite simple.[12] It is night in the desert and the North European travelers have reached an oasis. One strays from the group and finds himself surrounded by a pack of jackals who harass him; they appear at times wheedling and at times threatening. Forcing him to listen to their stories of hope and liberation, the jackals assure the traveler that he is their long-awaited savior. They tell him that he alone embodies their messianic hope; he only can free them from their masters, the Arabs. Freedom would be reached, they aver, if the traveler accepts to cut the Arabs' throats with a rusty pair of scissors. Should he succeed, explains the older jackal who is their leader, this will cleanse their whole nation, regain them pride and freedom. At this very moment, the Arab leader of the caravan who had been eavesdropping intervenes. He cracks his whip; the jackals disperse and wait at a distance.

The old Arab requests to retrieve the scissors. For him, the jackals are just "fools" who offer the same rusty scissors to every European who comes by. However, this does not prevent the Arabs from loving their jackals; they consider them their pets, dogs that are more beautiful than the European variety.[13] To demonstrate their true nature, the Arab has the carcass of a recently deceased camel brought to the cowering mass of jackals. Forgetting their previous concern with purity, the jackals pounce, let the camel's blood flow freely. In a huge, tumultuous heap, they tear at the camel's flesh, devouring the carcass ravenously. In their frenzied gluttony, they continue eating even as an Arab has begun whipping them.

Magnanimously, the European gestures to halt. The Arab desists, leaving the jackals to what he deems their "calling." At the end, the Arab praises the jackals in ambivalent terms: "Wonderful animals, aren't they? And how they hate us!"[14]

The text abounds in ironies and paradoxes. The jackals first pretend to have no fear of the Arabs, but they run away when a single old man cracks a whip. The jackals want to relieve the Arabs of their blood, but claim that they won't be able to kill them.[15] They roam the desert looking for free air and purity, yet they stink so horribly of carrion that the traveler nearly retches. They accuse the Arabs of killing animals and eating them like animals,[16] but they cannot resist the temptation of devouring a dead camel. Even the weapon they offer to the traveler is grotesquely inadequate for the task of slitting the throats of their masters: an old rusty pair of diminutive sewing scissors hanging from the fang of one of the jackals. What can this detail mean? Kafka's text is enigmatically precise in describing the weapon chosen by the jackals:

'Therefore, O master, therefore, dear, dear master, with the aid of your all-skillful hands, cut their throats with these scissors!' And at a jerk of his head a jackal came forward, carrying by his eye-tooth a small, age-rusted, pair of sewing scissors.[17]

One of the most accepted interpretations is that the jackals stand for the Jews and that Kafka ironizes their ancient purity rituals—a thesis defended most convincingly by Sander Gilman.[18] Gilman has shown that Kafka parodies the main Jewish rituals of cleanliness. The rusty scissors evoke the knife of the slaughter for shechita, the ritual slaughter defined by the dietary laws of Leviticus, or the mohel's blunt knife reserved for circumcision. The "purity" of the shechita rules would be the butt of Kafka's irony. Moreover, these rusty scissors also invoke the deliberate confusion between the instruments of circumcision and the accusations of ritual murder in the anti-Jewish propaganda. Of course, the joke is that the instrument chosen by jackals is a diminutive pair of tailor's scissors: in itself, the tool's shape necessitates fingers and hands, not fangs and paws, which is a good reminder of traditional Jewish disempowerment. A telling detail is that the scissors hang from a tooth, the only weapon available to jackals. Besides, being a tailor was one of the prototypical Jewish professions; the verb *schneiden* (to cut) used by the jackal for the expected murder is the usual German euphemism for circumcision. The Jewish tailor's guild sign was a hanging scissors very similar to the one mentioned in the story.[19]

We note another submerged pun when we read closely Kafka's term of *Nähschere*. In German, the verb *nähen* means to sew, but the noun *die Nähe* signifies proximity.[20] Thus *Nähschere* refers to the commonly used term of "sewing scissors" while referencing nearness: one of the levels of the tale refers to the traditional proximity of Jews and Arabs. Kafka shows them united by their ancient hatred, while having always practiced similar rituals like circumcision, the dietary laws excluding pigs and other unclean animals from licit food, the analogous linguistic origins. Besides, they all live in proximity to the desert, the place of exile and conquest.

Facing such dangerous nearness, it seems almost impossible to cut the Gordian knot of love and hatred, of admiration and execration. The text stages the impossibility of such a cut, which redoubles as the impossibility of there being a true Messiah. Like a human family, any text is a woven continuum in which one must cut (as Kafka knew with his practice of fragmentary writing and unfinished novels) to make sense. Here, the cut would have to do with the law, which is why the jackals feel the need for a cutting/circumcising savior. We understand that the choice of those jackals to represent the Jews in Palestine is not as absurd as it seemed at first. We know that the jackals living in these regions are not primarily predators but rather cowardly scavengers who eat dead and often decaying flesh, and readily devour the remains of others' feasts. Here, too, they require another to perform a murder as they recognize their impotence, their inability to free themselves.

The Bible often mentions jackals that live in ruins, and thus Job can say: "I have become a brother of jackals, a companion of owls" (Job 30:29). In the Middle East, jackals were venerated and linked with the dead. This was the role played by the Egyptian god Anubis, the jackal-headed god of the dead. The priests who performed the ritual embalming required for mummification wore Anubis-like masks on their heads. Freud's *Moses and Monotheism* presents monotheism as an Egyptian invention. In his reconstitution, the Jewish people were separated from their Egyptian ancestors by Moses who invented a history where his own Egyptian monotheism could be saved and revived. Freud owned a vividly colored *Frontal Covering of a Mummy* in which the text—an inscription that he had learned to decipher—stated: "May Anubis who is in his bandages, lord of the Sacred Land, come to you; may he give you a goodly burial."[21] When Kafka translates the Jews as jackals, it is because they partake of the same animal forms as their Egyptian ancestors who had lapsed back into polytheism.

The Jews find their lineage in generations that replace immortality with a matriarchal bloodline; the mother traditionally defines the Jewishness of a person. Accordingly, the old jackal alludes to mothers and not fathers when he declares: "I had almost given up hope, for we have been waiting for you an eternity; my mother waited for you, and her mother, and before her all their mothers, down to the mother of all jackals."[22] By turning the Jews into jackals, Kafka suggests that they are not so far from the archaic rituals that they aimed to repress in the name of the *Geistigkeit* that Freud extolled as the progress accomplished by Jewish monotheism, a word meaning both "intellectuality" and "spirituality."[23] Here is why the motif of blood is so important. This is launched almost inadvertently by the traveler who tells the jackals: "It seems to be a very ancient quarrel; so it might well be in the blood; and so perhaps it will only end in blood."[24] This leads the jackal leader to assume that the traveler is going to help them in their struggle against the Arabs who will be "relieved of their blood."

Clearly, here rust refers by metonymy to "blood." Indeed, medieval literature is replete with stories of knights who had to clean their swords to avoid corrosion by rust. In the earlier Homeric times, the heroes had bronze swords that would not rust, whereas iron and steel do. From the Greeks to the Romans, iron was always used for scissors. Here, the rust is said to be "ancient" (*mit altem Rost*), which calls up an "ancient blood." The paradox is that the tool of a liberation that will cleanse the perpetrators has been infected by obsolescence. Kafka knew Jewish legends speculating that Isaac had in fact been sacrificed by Abraham and not saved by God. The story of Isaac shows the dominance of the law of the father—by blood—over that of the mother's flesh. Freud had stressed how Jewish monotheism asserted the power of the father over the mother. Kafka's recurrent obsession—we see it at work in "The Judgment" and the series that he had planned to include "The Stoker"—was that there had to be a sacrifice of the son. Rust would be the stain that testifies to the fact that Isaac may not have been saved after all. As Freud noted, "The Mosaic religion had been a Father religion; Christianity became a Son religion."[25]

While rust is rarely mentioned in the Old Testament, it is often used in the New Testament as an example of earthly decay. The motif recurs in the Koran in which rust is described as sin tainting the clean radiance of the divine truth. We find in Koran 19, Surah Mutaffifin, those verses:

11. *Those who deny the Day of Judgment*

12. *And none denies it but every Transgressor, the Sinner!*

13. *When Our Signs are recited to him, he says: "Myths of the ancients."*

14. *Nay, Rather what they used to do has put rust upon their hearts.*

15. *Nay, most surely on That Day they shall be debarred from their Lord,*

16. *Then, they will enter the fire of Hell.*[26]

Such sinners believe that eschatology is made up of "ancient myths" and deny the existence of the day of the Judgment. Their denial is compared with rust on their hearts, for like rust, sin dulls the metallic light of divine revelation. The Koranic term of *ran* derives from *rayn* (rust). Rust in the Koran provides a neat metaphor for the process by which the radiance of truth vanishes when covered by a dull crust.

Kafka's story portrays the law as a foreign imposition—it comes from the whip of an Arab, someone who, we can assume, is a Muslim but will still refer to the God of Abraham and Isaac. As we have seen, Freud argued that Jewish monotheism was the invention of an Egyptian priest, Moses. If circumcision is not a defining factor here, its fictional instrument, those rusty scissors, might be. The practice of circumcision was shared by all Egyptians, a fact that surprised a Greek historian like Herodotus in the fifth century BC. Later, it became a sign of *islam* or "submission." At the beginning of Kafka's text, we view the jackals as beautiful in the movement of their bodies while also as submissive animals—"dark golden eyes gleaming, vanishing; slender bodies, as if under the whip compliant with a law, nimbly moving."[27] Quite deliberately, Kafka uses the Kantian term of *gesetzmässig:* "wie unter einer Peitsche gezetmässig."[28]

This text should be read next to another Kafkaian parable about failed messianism and the impossibility of accessing or addressing the law. It is the famous "In Front of the Law," a text first published in 1915 in another Jewish review, *Self-Defense (Selbstwehr),* to which Kafka would subscribe. At the time, *Self-Defense* was engaged in defining a strong Jewish identity and promoting Zionism. "In Front of the Law" was republished in a collection of avant-garde literature in 1917, and finally in Kafka's own 1919 collection, *A Country Doctor,* in which it just precedes "Jackals and Arabs."[29] The placement of the two stories implies a progression carefully calculated by Kafka. The deceptive logic of liberation attempted by animals that confirm their yoke all the more has been condensed in one Zürau aphorism: "The beast wrests the whip from the master and whips itself in order to become master, not knowing that this is only a fantasy produced by a new knot in the master's whip-lash."[30] Assuredly, the cunning Arab who wields his whip is not far, although it is unlikely that he would abandon his whip to the jackals. Here, the European appears as a disabused observer of the endless struggle between the whipping master and the deluded slave. The slave needs to believe in a Messiah—but the Messiah is anyone who happens to pass—and the belief confirms his subjection.

The great commentator of "In Front of the Law" was Jacques Derrida.[31] As Jacques Derrida acknowledged in "Circumfessions," his entire work can be considered as a meditation on the law and on circumcision, both perceived the mark of an alliance and a singular operation on one's body:

> Circumcision, that's all I've ever talked about, consider the discourse on the limit, margins, marks, marches, etc., the closure, the ring (alliance and gift), the sacrifice, the writing of the body, the pharmakos excluded or cut off, the cutting/sewing of Glas, the blow and the sewing back up, whence the hypothesis according to which it's that, circumcision, that, without knowing it . . . that I was always speaking or having spoken.[32]

Observing that in his family of Algerian Jews, they would say "baptism" for "circumcision," he admits of having suffered more or less consciously "of unavowable events, felt as such, not 'Catholic', violent, barbarous, hard, 'Arab', circumcised circumcision, interiorized, secretly assumed accusation of ritual murder."[33]

We began this chapter with von Hofmannsthal's diagnosis of a crisis in language. Signaling the end of a harmonious Platonician cosmos, rust was the symptom of an unbridgeable hiatus between Nature and Logos. The solution to the crisis perceived in 1902 was the invention of a new language, an idea which paved the way to modernist writers like Gertrude Stein, James Joyce, and Hermann Broch who, feeling a similar a language crisis, experimented with all the possibilities afforded by language. Kafka, falling prey to language crisis, unable to finish his texts, chose a different solution. For him, there had never been an originary harmony defining a cosmos. In contrast, aesthetics and ethical movements would function as divergent discourses; they might intersect when their chains of reasons would be knotted by a signifier like rust, a term whose precise meaning remained ambiguous. Apparently, then, Kafka did not experiment with language, which is why Samuel Beckett would (rather unfairly) criticize him, accusing him of an alleged timidity. Beckett told Israel Shenker in 1956: "Kafka's form is classic, it goes on like a steamroller—almost serene. It seems to be threatened the whole time—but the consternation is in the form. In my work there is consternation behind the form, not in the form."[34]

In fact, without subverting the surface of language, Kafka worked on it from within, as rust does. Playing on its fake obsolescence, Kafka lets language rust and then jokes about his rusty words. In the story we have discussed, Kafka undoes the threat of rust by exhibiting the rusty object and saturating it with meaning, to the point that it cannot be said to be either opaque or shining. But the rusty object reflects on what I had called in my childhood, quite simply, "Human Rust." At times, this reflection will generate panic or bafflement, and more often than not, a burst of laughter. "Simultaneously and alternately," we titter at a satire that cuts both ways and feel baffled. But this bafflement is pleasurable; we run like hamsters on a wheel, rehearsing carefully imbricated words; then, perhaps, will we feel touched by a sunray of rust; the ambivalent bliss it might cause, however, will be unable to ward off consternation.

5 RUST AESTHETICS

"Consternation" tends to suggest dismay and desolation. I had felt consternation at the disappearance of my tortoise, but the feeling of insuperable loss changed over time, especially when I imagined other sources of pastoral bliss for my vanished pet. Affects of loss and bereavement are often toned down or sublimated when subjected to the distancing agency of aesthetics. Kafka was keenly aware of an always possible reversal of ethics into aesthetics. The Austrian culture at the turn of the century, this slow and gay apocalypse, and the Japanese ideals founded on the ancient code of the samurai shared quite a few values—at least a concern for beauty in the face of imminent death.

In many ways, Kafka might have been a Chinese or a Japanese writer; he appeared rather exotic in his context at any rate. His last partner in Berlin, Dora Diamant, first thought he looked less like a Jew than "a half-blood Red Indian" given his swarthy complexion.[1] For me, Kafka's sensibility feels "Asian" in his concern for opaque allegories that use simple objects as their vehicle. His concern for obsolescence can also send us back to the concept of *sabi* introduced, as we saw in Chapter 1, by Paddy O'Reilly who mentions the term in the epigraph of her Australian novel *The Fine Color of Rust*. Explaining how she understands this word in an interview, she states: "I've spent quite a bit of time in Japan, and it was while I was talking to a Japanese friend that I remembered there is a word in Japanese for something that is often forgotten in the contemporary world. The word is *sabi*, and it describes an appreciation of imperfect and old things."[2] She was right to remind us of a concept that is elusive but still operative; it would not be foreign to the mental world of Kafka. If the term sends us back to an ancient aesthetics of imperfection and impermanence, it underpins themes and ideas that are alive in Japanese culture.

The term *sabi* is found in the *Manyōshū*, the eighth-century collection of Japanese poems (*Ten Thousand Leaves*), to evoke solitude. Later, "sabi" acquired the meaning of something that has grown "rusty" because of its similarity with a word with the same Romanization, *sabi* which means "rust." The main idea was that the object had aged and acquired a patina making it beautiful. Although the Japanese kanji characters 錆 (*sabi*, or "rust") and 寂 (*sabi*, or "desolation," and "loneliness") have different etymologies, the word as it was originally spoken was probably the same. Thus, *sabi* can be glossed as "beautiful imperfection." This is not a contradiction, for a pleasantly aged form will call up the passage of time. Calculated imperfection reminds us of the presence of mortality even in simple and homely objects like a tea cup; *sabi* things retain a link with the operation of time as aging and natural cycles perceived in the rhythm of the seasons. Thus, banal objects can be transfigured in spite of their diminished auras, perhaps because of their diminished auras, which anticipates themes treated by the *arte povera* movement in the second half of the twentieth century.

In Japan, the concept of *sabi* is associated with the works of the poet Matsuo Bashō (1644–94), who perfected the form of the haiku. Here is an example of a poem on the theme of *sabi*:

> *sabishisa ya*
> *kugi ni kaketaru*
> *kirigirisu*

This might be rendered as: "On the wall of the empty reception hall /A cage is hung / Crickets softly hum in the fall."[3] The word, *Sabishisa*, a term derived from the adjective *sabishi*, calls up "loneliness" in Japanese literature. Bashō often uses the word in close relationship with the spirit of quietude, *shizuka*, as in this variation:

> *shizukasa ya*
> *e kakaru kabe no*
> *kirigirisu*

> How quiet it is!
> On the wall where the painting hangs —
> A cricket.

The slightly different version (*sabishisa ya/kugi ni kaketaru/ kirigirisu*) I have quoted first could be translated as:

How solitary it is!
Hanging on a nail —
A cricket.

The cricket (*kirigirisu*), traditionally associated with the fall season, evokes loneliness and melancholy in classical Japanese poetry. A slightly longer poem about *sabi* deploys concrete examples. It is entitled, "Sabi is the color of haiku" (*sabi wa ku no iro nari*):

Sabi is the color of the poem.
It does not necessarily refer to the poem that describes a lonely scene.
If a man goes to war wearing a stout armor
or to a party dressed up in gay clothes,
and if he happens to be an old man, there is something lonely about him. Sabi is something like that.[4]

In Bashō's time, the word *sabi* had multiple meanings. Sam Hamill, one of the translators, writes that Bashō found in his travels the principle of lightness (*karumi*) allied with existential Zen loneliness, or *sabi*. It was their blending that generated "an elegantly understated, unpretentious natural beauty (*shibumi*)."[5] For Bashō, beauty derives from a sweet melancholia associated with the contemplation of objects that evoke impermanence.

One haiku highlights the theme of loneliness in the last page of *Narrow Road to the Interior*, Bashō's travelogue through Japan. This haiku (*sabishisa ya / suma ni kachi taru / hama no aki*) was composed on Iro beach, the "Colored Beach" north of Kyoto on the coast of the Sea of Japan. Translator Hiroaki Sato's rendering is:

> The loneliness here
> is superior to Suma,
> autumn on the beach.

Suma was reputed to be a desolate place, but Bashō and his friend found the *Iro no hama* beach to be even more forlorn; for them, the beach at dusk in the fall surpassed Suma in woeful loneliness. This poem marks the end of *Narrow Road to the Interior*, Bashō's celebrated five-month poetic trip. Suma calls up a chapter of the *Tale of Genji*, when an exiled Genji takes a boat to Suma, thereon marking it as a place of sad exile. Bashō and his companion saw the "Colored Beach" so permeated with desolation that they needed tea and hot sake to ward off the place's contagious melancholy.

Bashō's fame and literary legacy spliced the two concepts of *wabi* and *sabi*. Originally, *wabi* (侘) meaning "despondence," and *sabi* (寂), as we have seen, "solitude," taken together connote negative feelings while giving shape to a new refined aesthetic sensibility. At the time Europe experienced a craze for "china" porcelain, those imported polished glazed bowls and vessels that were admired and imitated in Portugal, Spain, England, and France, Japan was going in another direction, taking, as a new model, the rustic and less accomplished stoneware used by peasants and often associated with Korea. This led to the concept of imperfection turned into a supreme virtue. This defines the *sabi* concepts that were applied to the tea ceremony. The "way of tea" as developed by tea master Murata Shukō (1423–1502), who founded one of the first schools of tea ceremony, used only *sabi* tools and bowls. The ceremony, brought to perfection by Sen no Rikyū (1522–1591), was so contentious that Sen no Rikyū lost his life over a discussion of its rituals. Traditionally, tea ceremonies take place in small, rustic houses covered with a thatch roof; here is the place where the English rhyme of "rustic" and "rust" comes alive with a vengeance.

Closer to us, Junichirō Tanizaki's *In Praise of Shadows*, originally published in 1933, celebrates the idea of *sabi* in a modern context. Rejecting a Western tendency to present clean and shiny surfaces uniformly lit by powerful lamps, his Japanese sensibility will always opt for "a pensive luster" instead of "a shallow brilliance." Tanizaki loves the "murky light that, whether in a stone or an artifact, bespeaks a sheen of antiquity."[6] This ancient patina has nothing to do with the bright and glossy surfaces that we associate with perfect finish in products of modern technology. Tanizaki praises ancient and natural materials like wood or paper dimly lit by flickering lamps, especially in traditional Japanese toilets: "Yet for better or worse we do love things that bear the marks of grime, soot, and weather, and we love the colors and the sheen that call to mind the past that made them."[7] *Sabi* condenses an aesthetics of worn, dull, broken, and imperfect objects. Zen specialist Horst Hammitzsch comments: "The concept *sabi* carries not only the meaning 'aged'—in the sense of 'ripe with experience and insight' as well as 'infused with the patina that lends old things their beauty'—but also that of tranquility, aloneness, deep solitude."[8]

If *wabi* refers to philosophical concepts, *sabi* defines the materiality of objects rooted in time. *Wabi* evokes poverty, not just in the sense of an absence of material possessions but of things that look simple and devoid of ornament. The principles informing *wabi* combine Confucian, Taoist, Buddhist, and Shintoist themes, all of which spurn Western materialism. One main theme is that, in order to become more authentic, one should appreciate life's evanescence. This meditation on time and things, which could have an equivalent in the philosophy of Heidegger, is founded on a principle of subjective harmony with nature.

Sabi defines objects that are somewhat ambiguous in their shapes. These qualities are exemplified by ancient tea bowls and ceramics exhibited in the Nezu Museum in Tokyo.[9] Gallery Five displays tea artifacts that testify to the enduring values of *sabi*. A tea bowl called *Ko'ori—warikōdai* from the Korean Choson dynasty in the sixteenth century appears old, unglazed, and battered, which is unsurprising given the object's age; but it was designed in this way. A tea bowl with geometric patterns from the Japanese Momoyama-Edo period in the seventeenth century has a spherical silhouette. On closer inspection, it is a rough square battered into a circle. This *Nezumi Shino* ware has been shaped and coated in an iron slip into which designs were scraped and scratched. White glaze would sink into the scraped areas, creating a translucent relief. A slightly later *mukōzuke* food dish with geometric designs from the eighteenth-century Edo period presents a thick underglaze for which a mixture of cobalt and iron was poured on the bottom. The result is a dark rusty color in the inside, which exemplifies the combined criteria of *sabi*.

Sabi objects tend to be asymmetrical, age-worn, and unpretentious. The principles of *sabi* apply not only to tea huts, poetry, ceramics, calligraphy, tea ceremony, flower arranging, bonsai, archery, but also to music and theater. In all these cultural manifestations predicated on a broad sense of "rust," concepts of impermanence, humility, unconformity, and imperfection blend. The enjoyment of the transient physical qualities of the natural world derives from the perception that these objects allegorize finitude; here is a world in which, as Wallace Stevens stated, "Death is the mother of beauty." This imperfect beauty has little to do with Western canons, unless one looks at contemporary art after surrealism and Italian *arte povera*. Indeed, such an elegantly understated beauty can be discovered in surrealist "found objects" from flea markets, in rustic, half-broken, partly ruined, even decayed objects. A melancholic glow surrounds objects defined by their brittle impermanence, which cannot be reduced to today's trivialized concept of "shabby chic," although it shares some features with it.

On the whole, *Wabi-sabi* is the opposite of today's sleek, mass-produced, industrial artifacts offering a choice between fake immortality and rapid technological obsolescence. To abuse an old couple, *wabi-sabi* debunks the ideals of the technological sublime with its frail and tainted beauty. It reminds us that the contemporary sublime, as we have seen with Le Corbusier, cannot now be dissociated from the aesthetics of deindustrialization. *Sabi* looks back to pre-industrialization, to the passing of the seasons, to the biological time of our aging bodies—not to a history of shocks and awe facing massive destruction—and forward to a postindustrial aesthetics allegorized by cracks in enamel, frayed edges on sleeves, rust spots on instruments. It has been adapted by numerous artists working with ceramics; such is the case of Romy Northover, a British potter active in Brooklyn, who has found inspiration in *wabi-sabi* and offers an apt summary: "In Western culture we're always striving to see how close the hand can get to the precision of a machine, but once you create something immaculate, where do you go from there? Imperfection, on the other hand, has no limits."[10]

This sense of a limitless exploration shows that the rusty/rustic aesthetic is alive today in the Western world, as it is, as one could expect, in Japan. One can verify this by looking at the avant-garde fashion produced by Yohji Yamamoto, who has been faithful to the principle for several decades. All these abstract concepts sprang to life for me when I visited Yamamoto's main store in Tokyo.[11] Its huge doorframes encased in heavy metal are purposefully rusty; the big bay windows are covered with white paint crosses, as if lifted from recent construction sites. Many items of clothing I saw were inspired by rust. I thus discovered Yamamoto's "Men's Purple Burgundy and Rust Zipped Floral Blazer" along with the series of accessories, scarves, bags, and purses coming under the heading of "Discord," all inspired by photographs of smoke. The images of "Discord" are whirling smoke rings suggesting floating jellyfish or ephemeral flowers. The "imperfect beauty" of these accessories combines "transience" as our ontological fate and "restraint" as a creative understatement. Yohji Yamamoto, one of the fashion designers who represent Japan abroad, still disseminates the principle of *sabi*.

I will move away from Japan and visit Denmark, another important site for design and fashion. Among artists and architects who use rust in their creations, I will single out Knud Holscher in his work for the University of Odense in the central island of Funen. In 1966–67, Knud Holscher of KHR Arkitekter won an open competition to design the buildings and campus of the newly founded university of Odense. The work began in 1971 and lasted until 1976. The overall effect is stunning. The buildings are modernist, angular slabs of gray concrete for the most part, but the exterior walls and the passages linking one building to another are covered with huge weathering steel plates. As a result, given the wet climate, the metal is quick to rust. These steel plates have a life span of approximately forty years; many have already been replaced. Given the prevalence of rusty walls, the students of what is officially called the "University of Southern Denmark" have named their daily newspaper *Rust*. The university itself has been nicknamed "*Rustenborg*," or "The Castle of Rust."

The university design is relentlessly modern, with an accretive building system that allows for limitless growth. It is still growing. Even the neighbors have grown accustomed to seeing rust lying around in the countryside. The general effect is to mitigate harsh functionalism by referencing the seasons and the passing of time. What is superb is the contrast between the rust of the steel and the lush green grass. This contrast provides a soothing effect, both starkly modernist, constructivist even, with an added elemental twist. We are reminded of the proximity between metal and grass, both appearing as natural phenomena—the iron bleeding quietly into the grass, the grass accepting this metallic dissolution as a color complement to its green sympathy. Here might be a perfect realization of Ruskin's dream. Ruskin imagined ideally rusting leaves of iron in an English landscape as the homeliest proof that the interpenetration of nature and culture gave a moral lesson.[12] The architects also wanted to honor Hans Christian Andersen, the famous author of fairy-tales born in Odense. In 2009, Bjørn Nørgaard unveiled his monumental Hans Christian Andersen statue, with its three heads and a twisted tangle of limbs, the whole sculpture done in rusty colored bronze. The rather unflattering statue dominates the main square of the town. In Andersen's tale *The Old Street Lamp*, a magically animated lamp was endowed with the power of "falling into decay from rust whenever it pleased."[13] Soon, the lamp eschews the use of this suicidal power and prefers being passed from hand to hand, thus rusting away slowly and evenly. Rust provides a symbol for the generations of students passing through the buildings: they are reminded that time is short, that ultimately iron, grass, the buildings, and their lives will be mixed up in the same compost.

Several artists represent rust as an organic form via the medium of oxidizing iron. The most explicit work might be Julian Voss-Andreae's *Heart of Steel (Hemoglobin)*, a large-scale model of hemoglobin with a heart in the middle. Most of open-air sculptures made by Voss-Andreae interact with beautiful, natural surroundings in which they become progressively corroded.[14] The power of such monuments to rust becomes more dramatic when they bridge the gap between biology and history, as what one sees in the center of the British city of Coventry. Coventry was nearly bombed out of existence by the German Air Force on November 14, 1940. Two-thirds of the city and the cathedral were obliterated in one night. A moving *art brut* installation in front of the cathedral of Coventry commemorates the destruction: it is comprised of huge slabs of rusting steel vertically inserted into the ground that keep the names of the raid's victims alive. Here again, the aesthetics of rust emerge at the cusp between destruction and reconstruction. Closer to us, it was a mixture of rust and blood that served as an improvised ink for a screed testifying to atrocities: a precious list of eighty-two prisoners kept incognito in a Syrian jail was passed by Mansour Omani to the outside world; the list had been written on scraps of cloth with a makeshift ink combining blood from the prisoners' ailing gums and rust scraped from the iron bars of the cells.[15]

A similar hesitation between memorialization and denunciation underpins the work of Gal Weinstein, an Israeli artist born in 1970, who began his career using rusty steel wool glued on paper or plywood. This was the technique employed for the five "Dust Cloud" paintings from 2009, with steel wool on paper mounted on plywood, a series that I saw in Jerusalem in 2014.[16] The series includes images of tsunamis and catastrophes: one witnesses more than the dust that invades Jerusalem whenever the wind blows from the desert, for these dust clouds evoke the mushroom shapes of nuclear bombs or wartime explosions.

What struck me then was how Weinstein worked with steel wool as a substitute for drawing or photography. His slender and tiny metallic fibers are glued on a flat surface, which contributes to a photographic effect. Meanwhile they keep on rusting—time, caught in a snapshot, also works on the material work implied by the slow technique, the tedious act of gluing each fiber. Weinstein describes this process: "The transformation of the speed of the event and its documentation through the slow act of gluing contribute an attempt to prolong the experience of time and draw out a minute into days."[17] At the same time, the cheap and mass-produced material (steel wool) somehow mimics the use of *sanguine* or red chalk in classical portraits like Leonardo da Vinci's famous self-portrait in *sanguine*, but in a self-consciously postindustrial mode. Thus, we have a few self-portraits of the artist using the same medium: rusty steel wool on paper. As Weinstein said, this technique flirted with organic materials, and reminded him of fuzzy hairs adhering to paper in what he calls his "unshaven paintings," in a neat evocation of Marcel Duchamp's joke about his bearded and mustached Mona Lisa, that he later released in her natural state, but as he quipped, "shaved."[18]

Weinstein's elaborate interaction with time thanks to the medium of rusting metal turned monumental in his installation for the 2017 Venice Biennale. Weinstein, who represented Israel for the Biennale, proposed "Sun Stand Still," a massive artwork mixing several media calling up, by countless quotes, his previous works. Through painting, photography, video, and sculpture, the installation on three levels explores a precise political situation. The title refers to the Biblical miracle that allowed Joshua to destroy his enemies at the outcome of a victorious battle. Joshua Bin Nun was granted by God an extra day to slay the armies of the five Amorite kings at Gideon (Josh. 10:12-14). Using this biblical miracle as a point of departure, Weinstein shows that we are caught up between the chaos of the organic world and the impossibility of waking up from the recent nightmares of history. "Sun Stand Still," on view from May to November 2017 in the Israeli Pavilion at the Venice Biennale, meditates on art's desire to stop time. The installation also critically engages with the romantic images of Zionist colonization that are deeply embedded in Israel's collective memory.

The central axis of the installation—"Moon over Ayalon Valley"—evokes the biblical miracle in a negative manner. The beautiful modernist pavilion is turned into a site that suggests desolate, moldy, and decaying rooms. "Jezreel Valley in the Dark," the floor installation on the intermediate level, consists of a puzzle-shaped arrangement of agricultural plots filled with rotting coffee dregs that are slowly invaded by mold (one can smell the pungent mold in all the rooms). Weinstein quotes his earlier "Black Coffee" (2013) made with steel wool and wool glued on plywood, and his 2002 "Vacuuming (Jezreel Valley)," an installation in which the legendary fertile fields were figured as a jigsaw puzzle of carpets that could be vacuumed at will. The parallel elimination of dust and the domination of rust call up the bloody elimination of the inhabitants of Canaan by Joshua, who, we may remember, slaughtered all—men, women, and children—of the enemies he found there in his victorious military campaign.

In Venice, Weinstein has reproduced an "agricultural laboratory" that ironically inverts the way the desert was conquered by Israeli colons. Here, maintenance and dynamism have been replaced by ruin, inaction, and neglect. This bitter satire reminds us that biblical chronicles teemed with "miracles" or more precisely religious wars that spelled out absolute destruction, if not always ethnic cleansing. The divine miracle in the Ayalon Valley echoes the Zionist project of conquering the barren wilderness of Palestine based on blind faith in religious election and technological progress. The top floor sculpture, called "El Al," the name of Israel's national airline, and the injunction to go upward in Hebrew, fills the room and represents the clouds of smoke and fire just after a missile has been fired.

There is no escaping the vision of contemporary conflicts between Israelis and Arabs, triggered of course by the Palestinian issue. Taken together, these rusty, wooly, and moldy objects evoke a postapocalyptic and postindustrial vision, a bitter satire of the Zionist dreams of colonization and expansion. By showing that something is rotten in the kingdom of Israel, Weinstein exposes the terrible cost of human or divine hubris, showing the dangers of a conquest made in the name on a theocratic political vision. The doubling of rust and dust, allied with the use of moldy coffee dregs, calls up the biological and organic sense of "rust," that old parasite of coffee leaves, discussed in Chapter 1. Sun may stand still—but "rust never sleeps." Or, as Freud reminded us in *Moses and Monotheism* (as we saw in connection with Kafka's tale of Arabs and jackals), the sun that stops if God grants it may well have been an Egyptian invention, if it is the sun of Aton, the first monotheistic god.[19]

CONCLUSION: FOUGÈRES TO MARSEILLES: GREEN RUST OR EDIBLE *ROUILLE*?

Gal Weinstein's toxic mixtures, propped on rusting steel wool and rotten coffee dregs, dispersed mold spores throughout the Israeli pavilion at the Venice Biennale. This aggressive artistic gesture recalls ecological disasters and other postindustrial apocalypses. However, by insisting on the biological aspect of the different modes of corrosion, Weinstein points in another direction; his work is looking to a different future. He suggests that some hope is to be expected from our own bodily interactions with biological transformations, whatever the basis of these metamorphoses. New ecological vistas have appeared since the turn of this century when scientists started working on applications of rust, including what is called "green rust." New hope has been generated: many propose that these forms of "rust" will remedy various types of pollution. Indeed, already some rusts can absorb, degrade, or contain metallic remainders of industrial pollution, undoing years of damage. Rusts tend to negate the entropy associated with industrial pollution.

Green rust had long been observed as a specific form of corrosion on iron and steel surfaces; we now know that it can be found in nature under the shape of the mineral "fougèrite," named for its recent discovery in an ancient forest near Fougères, Brittany, France. Blue-green or blue-gray in color, it takes the form of a clay-like mineral shaped in hexagonal platelets of submicron diameter. Similar minerals are present in water-logged soils and sediments. Due to their high reactivity, green rusts play an important role in the destruction of contaminants in soils, sediments, and aquifers. They might soon be applied to water and gas purification. For instance, due to its ability to transform inorganic contaminants, green rust could remediate the chlorinated hydrocarbon pollution associated with pesticides. At last, the reduction of polluting elements would be achieved by a natural process.

Another fascinating development of science derives from a closer examination of the biology of specific iron-feeding bacteria. The research of David Emerson at the Bigelow Laboratory for Ocean Sciences is exemplary. The laboratory's YouTube channel has relayed his findings and those of colleagues like Roger Griffith and Louis Powtoon.

I'll quote a passage from a conversation that sheds light on the wonderful new frontiers they are exploring. Here, David Emerson discusses the effects of an organism called *Leptothrix ochracea*, an iron-oxidizing bacteria that has been feeding on iron in water for three billion years. Similar organisms are considered a nuisance because they foul and corrode water pipelines.

> Ari: There have been episodes—in Berlin and Beijing, for example—when people turned on their taps and orange water gushed out.
>
> Emerson: The entire system had gotten clogged with iron bacteria.
>
> Ari: But they're not all bad. Once the bacteria feed on the iron, it turns to rust, and that rust can grab onto stuff floating by—like arsenic, other harmful metals, even viruses. In other words, these bacteria can actually help filter water. And that rust—it's remarkably delicate.
>
> Field: We have this nice, fluffy, light orange matte. Like if you pulled out part of a pillow, it kinda reminds me of that. But then, you see within it, we have this really dark orange, almost looks like crumble topping, kinda like on a coffee cake.
>
> Ari: So, in other words, in this ditch, we're looking at an incredibly complicated ecosystem. . . . Emerson says it's just a matter of time before we figure out how to harness these bacteria to improve our world—by

filtering water, building mini-structures out of rust, and catalyzing reactions. Not bad for a group of bacteria dining on iron in a roadside ditch.[1]

This is a domain whose untold applications remain to be explored. It shows that, as Bertrand Russell stated, the main riddle facing us is not the human mind, but matter—what science tells us about matter's properties is more productive and imaginative than any introspective speculation about the psyche. Or, if we listen to thinkers coming from a different horizon, like French philosopher Maurice Merleau-Ponty, the theoretical task for the future would be to connect our psyches to these properties of matter, once we understand them. In his later seminars, Merleau-Ponty elaborated a philosophy of Nature that echoes these concerns, since, for him, human beings and the world are linked by a principle of rationality in which one discerns traces of a common language or Logos:

> Neither a theory of knowledge nor a metascience seeking the substance of physical Nature of the organism.
>
> But, across the movement of science, to open unto the placing in question of the Being-object of Nature, unto the Nature that "we are," unto the Nature in us—and thereby to begin a revision of the ontology of the object, a fortiori, since the leaf of nature detaches from the object and rejoins our total being.[2]

As we have seen, rust appears both in the outside world as a consequence of processes like rain and wind, and in our bodies through the redness of our blood and its curious irritability. Would this double "nature" testify to the common Logos Merleau-Ponty supposes? This Logos would be a code of Nature allowing us to understand its link with human language. In the case of rust, there would be a Logos of endless combustion and regeneration, a material language of metallic corrosion and biological recycling. Language is a virus, William Burroughs would say; thus, we could envisage a new version of the *logos spermatikos*, which, for the Stoics, was the generative principle of the Universe, creating and destroying all things, a principle underpinned by a general seminal rationality: *logos spermatikos* would be rewritten as *logos skouriatikos*, the rationality of corrosion doubling as generation. As Merleau-Ponty argues, we must understand the knotting between the flesh of the world and our bodies: "The flesh of the body makes us understand the flesh of the world."[3] What if rust were more than mere industrial rubbish—instead, a living and dynamic environment linking our lives with the world? What if it showed us how to absorb the world, not simply to process it intellectually, but also to devour it? Finally, if rust can eat industrial pollution, we can also eat rust.

"Rust" in French is *rouille*, as we know. It is the name of a delicious sauce that accompanies *bouillabaisse*, the fish soup served in Marseille's restaurants—originally a poor fishermen's dish made of bones and heads, the remainders of partly eaten or unsold fish. The dish goes back to the seventh century BC, when the city of Massalia founded by Greek settlers developed its distinct identity and named that soup *kakavia*. To be user-friendly, I'll offer my recipe for *rouille*. No true *bouillabaisse* can come without an adequate *rouille*. In Marseille, everyone has an "authentic" recipe for *rouille*. Here is one I like, for four to eight people. Start with a base of potato boiled in the fish stew. Add four sea bream livers (they provide most of the color and flavor; in fact, almost any fish liver will do if you cannot find sea bream) and three urchin gonads, all also previously boiled in the stew. Follow with two red peppers, two garlic cloves, five spoonfuls of olive oil, a pinch of salt, and a whole spoonful of saffron. In a mortar, crush the peppers along with salt and garlic. Add the boiled potato and mash it. Warm up the bream livers and the urchin gonads before mixing them in the paste. Pour the olive oil and beat the mixture up so as to create an emulsion. Sprinkle with pepper.[4] *Rouille* with its signature hue, the rusty color, provides a perfect accompaniment for any soup, delicious if you spread it on toasted bread. *Bon appétit!*

Appetite for rust? That *is* food for thought . . . "Thought of what?" you might ask. We've spoken of metal corrosion— does this mean less metal, or more metal? Is it scarcity or excess that we are after? Remember: insomniac rust is the exact opposite of rest. Don't rest in peace, but enjoy what's still edible in our world. Think about my previous vignettes, my travelogues, all aiming at showing and telling. I tried to present not just lessons in lessness but to clarify and also complicate my chosen object. My complication/clarification effort would ultimately rely on Merleau-Ponty's knotting of "Logos" with "Nature." Here would be a task for thought: to gain a better sense of the infinitely restless dialectics of Nature.

ACKNOWLEDGMENTS

I want to thank Haaris Naqvi for his trust and friendship, Scott Jenkins for his expertise in matters of technology and hemoglobin, and Ashley Stinnett, who reread the manuscript, for her superb sense of style.

Illuminating conversations with Eri Miyawaki, Manya Steinkoler, and Peter Szendy helped me make better sense of certain texts I discuss.

Constraints of space prevented the inclusion of a section on the "music of rust" discussing Neil Young's 1979 song "Rust Never Sleeps" and the 1995 founding of the heavy metal band Rusty Eye in Mexico City. Rusty Eye's *Saca El Cobre* (2014), played loud, can provide a solid accompaniment to Chapter 1.

NOTES

Introduction

1 Henri Rabaté, *Glossaire trilingue, français-anglais-allemand, spécial aux industries des cires, huiles, gommes, résines, pigments, vernis, encres, peintures, produits d'entretien et préparations assimilées* (Paris, 1949).

2 *"This England is so Different": Italo Svevo's London Writings*, tr. and eds. John Gatt-Rutter and Brian Moloney (Market Harborough: Troubador, 2003).

3 See *"This England is so Different": Italo Svevo's London Writings*, p. 24, for a letter in which he plans to give up smoking—which he never did. This promise that he never fulfilled became a major leitmotif in Svevo's most famous novel, *Zeno's Conscience*.

4 The work was realized by Shinslab Architecture for the Seoul edition of MoMA's Young Architects Program, a team led by architect Shin Hyung-Chul Tchely in collaboration with Claire Shin, Charles Girard, Souho Lee, Camille Chalverat, Javier García González, and Taewoo Ha. See https://www.dezeen.com/2016/07/20/shinslab-architecture-rusty-ship-transformed-cavernous-pavilion-momas-young-architects-program-yap-seoul/.

5 Le Corbusier, *Towards a New Architecture*, tr. Frederick Etchells (New York: Dover, 1986), 92.

6 See the chapter "The Deindustrial Sublime," in Steven High and David W. Lewis, *Corporate Wasteland: The Landscape and Memory of Deindustrialization* (Ithaca, NY: ILR Press, 2007), 23–39.

7 One example is François Bon's descriptive exercise, *Paysage Fer (Iron Lanscape)* (Paris: Verdier, 2000), a beautifully written book whose narrator attempts to "exhaust" the postindustrial landscape in the "rust belt" in the East of France. Going back and forth from Paris to Nancy, Bon lists abandoned mills, old factories, empty railway stations, but not once uses the word "rust." There is only one passing reference to "oxidized corrugated sheets," p. 61.

8 Jonathan Waldman, *Rust: The Longest War* (New York: Simon and Schuster, 2015).

9 Allen Dieterich-Ward, *Beyond Rust: Metropolitan Pittsburgh and the Fate of Industrial America* (Philadelphia: University of Pennsylvania Press, 2016).

Chapter 1

1 I am using the account provided by Rolf E. Hummel in *Understanding Materials Science: History, Properties, Applications*, 2nd ed. (New York: Springer, 2004), 155–58.

2 Paul Hertneky, *Rust Belt Boy: Stories of an American childhood* (Peterborough: Bauhan Publishing, 2016), 13. Hereafter RBB and page number.

3 RBB, p. 14.

4 RBB, p. 25.

5   RBB, p. 31.

6   Philipp Meyer, *American Rust* (New York: Spiegel and Grau, 2010), 16.

7   P. A. O'Reilly, *The Fine Color of Rust* (New York: Washington Square, 2012), 150. Hereafter FCR and page number.

8   FCR, p. 2.

9   FCR, p. 276.

10 FCR, n. p.

11 "The Oxidation of the documentary: The politics of rust in Wang Bing's *Tie Xi Qu, West of the Tracks*," in *Third Text, Critical Perspectives on Contemporary Art and Culture* 29, no. 1–2 (2015): 1–13. Abbreviated as OD and page number.

12 OD, p. 2.

13 OD, p. 9.

14 OD, p. 9.

15 OD, p. 10.

16 OD, p. 12.

17 Roland Barthes, *Camera Lucida: Reflections on Photography*, tr. Richard Howard (New York: Farrar, Straus, and Giroux, 1981); and Kaja Silverman, *The Miracle of Analogy, or The History of Photography, Part 1* (Stanford: Stanford University Press, 2015).

18 Wang Bing in an interview for the *New Left Review* 82 (July–August 2013), 124.

19 *Télérama*, November 28, 2011; Jérémie Couston, "Un cinéaste au fond des yeux #122: Wang Bing, réalisateur de "Three Sisters," www.telerama.fr/.../un-cineaste-au-fond-des-yeux-122-wang-bing-.

20 Georges Didi-Huberman, *Peuples Exposés, Peuples Figurants, L'Oeil de l'Histoire, 4* (Paris: Editions de Minuit, 2012), 235–57;

and the lecture on "Hors-je, *L'Homme sans nom*," Centre Pompidou, https://www.centrepompidou.fr/id/c8ELXyR/ra8BL6/fr.

21 Didi-Huberman, *Peuples Exposés, Peuples Figurants*, 256.

22 See Mark Wang, Zhiming Cheng, Pingyu Zhang, Lianjun Tong, and Yanji Ma, eds., *Old industrial Cities Seeking New Road of industrialization: Models of Revitalizing Northeast China* (Singapore: World Scientific Publications, 2014), 77.

23 Ibid., 88.

24 J. M. Coetzee, "Two Interviews," *Triquarterly* 69 (1987): 455.

25 J. M. Coetzee, *Life & Times of Michael K* (New York: Penguin, 1983), 115. Hereafter abbreviated as LT and page number.

26 See the film stills reproduced by Didi-Huberman in *Peuples Exposés, Peuples Figurants*, p. 236, 237, and 251.

27 LT, p. 59.

28 LT, p. 113.

29 LT, p. 114.

30 LT, p. 117.

31 LT, p. 138.

32 LT, p. 139.

33 Plato, *The Collected Dialogues*, eds. Edith Hamilton and Huntington Cairns (Princeton: Princeton University Press, 1996), *The Republic*, III, 415de, 659.

34 See Marc Shell, *Children of the Earth: Literature, Politics and Nationhood* (New York: Oxford University Press, 1993).

35 LT, p. 154.

36 Nadine Gordimer, "The Idea of Gardening," February 2, 1984, *New York Review of Books*, http://www.nybooks.com/articles/1984/02/02/the-idea-of-gardening/.

37 Walter Benjamin, *The Arcades Project*, tr. H. Eiland and K. McLaughlin (Cambridge, MA: Harvard University Press, 1999), 329. Hereafter abbreviated as AP and page number.

38 J. M. Coetzee, "Walter Benjamin, the Arcades Project" (2001) in *Inner Workings: Literary Essays 2000–2005* (New York: Viking, 2007), 63–64.

39 In the *Arcades Project*, Benjamin often quotes Sigfried Giedion's 1928 classic *Building in France, Building in Iron, Building in Ferroconcrete*. In that book, Giedion expresses only praise for the modern use of cast iron and then steel for buildings in France and elsewhere.

40 Louis-Ferdinand Céline, *Death on the Installment Plan*, tr. Ralph Manheim (New York: New Directions, 1971), 116.

41 *Death on the Installment Plan,* 70–71.

42 Walter Benjamin, "Surrealism: The last snapshot of the European Intelligentsia," in *Selected Writings,* vol. 2, part 1, 1927–30, eds. Michael W. Jennings, Howard Eiland, and Gary Smith (Cambridge, MA: Harvard University Press, 1999), 210. Translation modified.

43 Ibid., 210.

Chapter 2

1 G. W. F. Hegel, *Philosophy of Nature*, tr. A. V. Miller (Oxford: Oxford University Press, 2004), § 330, *Zusatz*, 251. Abbreviated as PN and page number.

2 PN, p. 251.

3 Ibid.

4 Ibid.

5 PN, p. 244.

6 PN, p. 245.

7 PN, p. 238.

8 Ibid.

9 PN, p. 239.

10 PN, pp. 239–40.

11 PN, p. 241.

12 Markus Semm, *Der springende Punkt in Hegels System* (München: Boer, 1994). I owe this reference to Peter Szendy; see Peter Szendy, *A Coups de Points* (Paris: Minuit, 2013), 106–07.

13 PN, p. 366.

14 PN, p. 367.

15 PN, p. 368.

16 Ibid.

17 PN, p. 369.

18 Ibid.

19 Ibid.

20 Ibid.

21 Ibid.

22 PN, p. 392.

23 Ibid.

24 PN, pp. 392–93.

25 Jean-Luc Nancy, *Hegel: The Restlessness of the Negative*, tr. Jason Smith and Steven Miller (Minneapolis: University of Minnesota Press, 2002).

26 John Ruskin, *The Two Paths*, ed. Christine Roth (West Lafayette, IN: Parlor Press, 2004), 90. Hereafter, abbreviated as TP and page number.

27 TP, p. 92.

28 Ibid.

29 TP, p. 93.

30 Ibid.

31 Ibid.

32 Ibid.

33 Ibid.

34 TP, p. 94.

35 Ibid.

36 Ibid.

37 TP, p. 95.

38 Ibid.

39 Ibid.

40 TP, p. 96.

41 TP, p. 97.

42 Adrian Stokes, *Stones of Rimini* (1935), in *The Critical Writings*, vol. I, 1930–1937, ed. Lawrence Gowing (London: Thames and Hudson, 1978), 192. Hereafter SR and page number.

43 SR, pp. 191–204.

44 SR, p. 196.

45 Ibid.

46 SR, p. 197.

47 TP, p. 98.

48 Charles Darwin, *The Expression of the Emotions in Man and Animals* (Chicago: The University of Chicago Press, 1965), 309.

49 TP, p. 100.

50 TP, p. 99.

51 TP, p. 112.

52 TP, p. 114.

53 TP, p. 115.

54 Ibid.

55 John Ruskin, *Fors Clavigera,* Letter 7 on "Charitas," *The Works of John Ruskin, Library Edition* vol. XXVII, eds. E. T. Cook and Alexander Wedderburn (London: George Allen, 1907), 116.

56 *Fors Clavigera*, 122.

57 Marcel Proust, *Swann's Way*, tr. Lydia Davis (New York: Viking, 2002), 82–83.

58 *Fors Clavigera*, 130.

Chapter 3

1 Roland Barthes, "Steak-frites," *Mythologies*, tr. Richard Howard and Annette Lavers (New York: Hill and Wang, 2012), 83.

2 Roland Barthes, "Wine and Milk," *Mythologies*, 82.

3 See the chapter "Biochemistry of Hemoglobin," in *Hemoglobin-Based Oxygen Carriers as Red Cell Substitutes and Oxygen Therapeutics* (Springer, 2013), http://link.springer.

com/chapter/10.1007%2F978-3-642-40717-8_3.
I thank Scott Jenkins who has condensed these analyses
for me.

4 Franz Kafka, "The Wish to Be a Red Indian," tr. Willa and
Edwin Muir, in *The Complete Stories*, ed. Nahum N. Glazer
(New York: Schocken, 1971), 390.

5 Franz Kafka, "The Vulture," tr. Tania and James Stern, *The
Complete Stories*, 443.

Chapter 4

1 http://depts.washington.edu/ vienna/documents/
Hofmannsthal/ Hofmannsthal_Chandos.htm, accessed April
14, 2017, translation modified. I am quoting the unpaginated
text reproduced in this website. I signal when I modify the
translation. The German text is "Ein Brief von Hugo von
Hofmannsthal," at the Projekt Gutenberg website.

2 *The Letter* was published under the title of "Ein Brief" in
two consecutive issues of the Berlin newspaper *Der Tag*, on
October 18 and 19, 1902.

3 Hugo von Hofmannsthal, Leopold von Andrian,
Briefwechsel, ed. Walter H. Perl (Frankfurt: Fischer, 1968),
160.

4 Francis Bacon, *The Works of Francis Bacon*, ed. Basil Montagu
(London: Pickering, 1881, vol. 14), 314.

5 For an excellent treatment of allusions to Bacon in the "Letter,"
see Eric L. Santner's reading in *The Royal Remains: The People's
Two Bodies and the Endgame of Sovereignty* (Chicago: The
University of Chicago Press, 2011), 173–76.

6 J. M. Coetzee, *Elizabeth Costello* (New York: Penguin, 2003). Costello mentions the general assumption that Kafka's Red Peter in "Report to an Academy" is an allegory for the Jews who have to perform for the non-Jews, but she disagrees with this interpretation (p. 62). Then Costello contradicts the philosopher Thomas Nagel who stated that humans can never know how bats think and feel (pp. 75–80). The end of the novel rewrites von Hofmannsthal's "Letter," this time written and signed by Lady Chandos (pp. 227–30).

7 *Der Jude* 2, no. 7 (1917–18), 488–90.

8 "May I ask you not to call the pieces parables; they are not really parables. If they are to have any overall title at all, the best might be: 'Two animal stories.'" Letter to Martin Buber, May 12, 1917, in *Letters to Friends, Family and Editors*, tr. Richard and Clara Winston (New York: Schocken, 1977), 132.

9 I translate Franz Kafka, *Das dritte Oktavheft*, in *Hochzeitsvorbereitungen auf dem Lande und andere Prosa*, ed. Max Brod (Frankfurt: Fischer, 1983), 52. For a different rendering, see Reiner Stach, *Kafka: The Years of Insight*, tr. Shelley Frisch (Princeton: Princeton University Press, 2013), 178.

10 Franz Kafka, "The Collected Aphorisms," in *The Great Wall of China and Other Short Works*, ed. Malcolm Pasley (London: Penguin, 1991), 79. Abbreviated as GWC.

11 I discuss this in *Crimes of the Future: Theory and Its Global Reproduction* (New York: Bloomsbury, 2014), 177–79.

12 I am quoting Joyce Crick's translation in Franz Kafka, *A Hunger Artist and Other Stories* (Oxford: Oxford University Press, 2012), 22–25. Abbreviated as HA and page number.

13 HA, p. 24.

14 HA, p. 25.

15 HA, p. 23.

16 *fressen* is the verb used, HA, p. 22.

17 HA, p. 24. The German text has: "*schneide ihnen mit dieser Schere die Hälse durch!" Und einem Ruck seines Kopfes folgend kam ein Schakal herbei, der an einem Eckzahn eine kleine, mit altem Rost bedecked Nähschere trug*." Franz Kafka, *Ein Landartzt und andere Prosa* (Stuttgart: Reclam, 1995), 24. Hereafter abbreviated as EL and page number.

18 Sander Gilman, *Franz Kafka: The Jewish Patient* (New York: Routledge, 1995), 150–52.

19 There are countless Jewish jokes alluding to exchanges between the instruments of circumcision and tailors' scissors. Other jokes refer to the impossibility of advertising for *mohels* who perform the circumcision. One of my favorite versions (it has many variations) is this: Samuel spends the night in a hotel in a small town in Galicia. As he has to take a train early in the morning and his alarm clock has stopped working, he goes looking for a watch repair store. Soon he finds one with a big clock sign hanging over the door. Inside, he is greeted by a man who tells him that he cannot repair clocks, for he is a mohel. Samuel asks: "But then why do you have a clock on the sign over your door?" "What would you want me to hang out there—a schmock?"

20 I am indebted to Manya Steinkoler for this remark and other astute comments on the story.

21 See Janine Burke, *The Sphinx on the Table: Sigmund Freud's Art Collection and the Development of Psychoanalysis* (New York: Walker and Co., 2006), 228.

22 HA, p. 22.

23 Sigmund Freud, *Moses and Monotheism* (New York: Random House, 1967), 142.

24 HA, p. 23.

25 Freud, *Moses and Monotheism*, 111.

26 https://www.al-islam.org/enlightening-commentary-light-holy-quran-vol-19/surah-mutaffifin-chapter-83. Accessed April 16, 2017.

27 HA, p. 22, modified.

28 EL, p. 22.

29 For the complex publication history that changes the nature of the text and of its interpretation by Derrida, see Howard Caygill, "Kafka and Derrida *Before the Law*," in *Freedom and Confinement in Modernity: Kafka's Cages,* eds. A. Kiarina Kordela and Dimitris Vardoulakis (New York: Palgrave, 2011), 48–59.

30 Franz Kafka, *The Great Wall of China and Other Short Works*, tr. and ed. Malcolm Pasley (London: Penguin, 1991), 83.

31 See Jacques Derrida, "Before the Law," in *Acts of Literature*, ed. Derek Attridge (New York and London: Routledge, 1992), 183–220.

32 Jacques Derrida, "Circumfession," in *Jacques Derrida*, eds. Geoffrey Bennington and Jacques Derrida (Chicago: The University of Chicago Press, 1993), 70–71.

33 Ibid., 73.

34 Quoted in Samuel Beckett, *The Critical Heritage*, eds. Lawrence Garver and Raymond Federman (London: Routledge, 1978), 148.

Chapter 5

1 Dora Diamant, "Mein Leben mit Franz Kafka," in *"Als Kafka mir entgegen kam," Erinnerungen an Franz Kafka,* ed. Hans-Gerd Koch (Berlin: Klaus Wagenbach, 2005), 194.

2 Interview accessible in paddyoreilly.com.au/wp-content/uploads/2011/12/reading-guide-FCOR.pdf.

3 I thank Eri Myawaki, Professor at Gakushuin University, Tokyo, for providing a translation and a gloss for this haiku.

4 *Classical Japanese Database*, Translation #42, translation by Robert Hass.

5 Matsuo Bashō, *Narrow Road to the Interior and other writings*, translated by Sam Hamill (Boston: Shambala, 1998), 169.

6 Junichirō Tanizaki, *In Praise of Shadows*, tr. Thomas J. Harper and Edward G. Seidensticker (London: Vintage Books, 2001), 20.

7 Tanizaki, *In Praise of Shadows*, 20.

8 Horst Hammitzsch, *Zen in the Art of the Tea Ceremony* (New York: Penguin, 1983), 46.

9 Nezu Museum, 6-5-1 Minami-Aoyama Minato-ku, Tokyo 107-0062, Japan. See the website http://www.nezu-muse.or.jp.

10 Quoted in Alexandra Brazilian, "Divine Imperfection," *New York Times Style Magazine*, (May 21, 2017), 78.

11 Yohji Yamamoto, Aoyama Main Store, 5-3-6 Minamiaoyama Minato-ku, 107-0062 Tokyo, Japan, visited in May 2017.

12 See Lars Spuybroek, *The Sympathy of Things: Ruskin and the Ecology of Design*, 2nd ed. (New York: Bloomsbury, 2016).

13 Hans Christian Andersen, *Stories for the Household* (New York: McLoughlin Brothers, 1893), 201.

14 See http://julianvossandreae.com/works/protein-sculptures-outdoor-works/.

15 Avantika Chilkoti, "From Syrian Prison, Cloth Scraps Immortalize Detainees' Names in Rust and Blood," *New York Times*, August 10, 2017, A 4.

16 See the catalog of the exhibition *Collecting Dust* in the Israel Museum of Jerusalem (December 2013 to April 2014), curated by Tamar Manor-Freidman.

17 *Collecting Dust* catalog (Jerusalem: The Israel Museum, 2013), 50.

18 Gal Weinstein and Jerzy Michalowicz, "Building Materials: An email conversation," in *Gal Weinstein: Huleh Valley* (Tel Aviv: Tel Aviv Museum of Art, 2005), 108.

19 See the excellent essay by Yair Zakovitch, "Sun Stand Still: Metamorphosis of a Miracle," in the catalog of the Israeli Pavilion Biennale Arte 2017, May 9 to November 26, 2017, 125–31. Weinstein's complex allegory is presented in a wonderful introductory essay by Tami Katz-Freiman, the curator of the installation, that would deserve being quoted in full, "Stopping Time, Stopping Mold," ibid., 37–63.

Conclusion

1 See http://theterramarproject.org/thedailycatch/iron-oxidizing-bacteria/.

2 Maurice Merleau-Ponty, *Nature: Course Notes from the College de France*, ed. Dominique Segland, tr. Robert Vallier (Evanston, IL: Northwestern University Press, 2003), 212–13. I have respected the inconsistent capitalization of Nature.

3 Merleau-Ponty, *Nature*, 218.

4 See the website http://la-cachina.over-blog.com/
article-17189722.html, for a similar recipe.

INDEX